THE TRUTH ABOUT CATS
AND DOGS

THE TRUTH ABOUT CATS AND DOGS

Emma Milne

Book Guild Publishing
Sussex, England

First published in Great Britain in 2007 by
The Book Guild Ltd
Pavilion View
19 New Road
BN1 1UF

Typesetting in Times by
Keyboard Services, Luton, Bedfordshire

Printed in Great Britain by
CPI Bath

A catalogue record for this book is available from
The British Library

ISBN 978 1 84624 137 6

For Emily, for her relentless faith in the book, for Mark for his unwavering love and support and for Margaret who never got to read how much she and Elgar meant to me.

Contents

Preface

Owing to many prolonged pauses this book has been seven years in the making. The final spur came from Emily, to whom the book is dedicated. My former mother-in-law, she is now a close friend. She loved the book from the first draft and has badgered me ever since about putting it before you, the public.

I qualified as a vet in 1996 from Bristol University and have worked all over the place since then. My first job was a very mixed practice on Exmoor. A move after a year took me to Cheltenham, where I stayed for almost seven years in three different practices. I now live near York with another vet and a motley crew of waifs and strays that I have picked up along the way.

During my time as a vet and also a vet student I have come across a startling number of wrongs and injustices in the way our dogs and cats are bred, as well as misconceptions on the part of the public about so-called 'pedigrees'. It is for this reason that I have written this book. I have also come to realise that I am not alone in these views, although sometimes it is easy to feel that way.

A couple of years ago I had the great privilege of meeting my absolute hero, Sir David Attenborough. A friend of mine from the BBC, Martin, was working with him on the dubbing of *Life of Mammals* and arranged for me to go and sit in on a session. I was like a nervous schoolchild and almost made excuses not to go; I was sure he would think me a complete idiot for idolising him to the extent I do. In reality, of course, I know he is only an 'ordinary' person, and as well as being a brilliant naturalist he is a generous and down-to-earth man. Fame is a very strange thing.

Nevertheless I could not give up this once-in-a-lifetime opportunity and I arrived clutching in hand the copy of *Life on Earth* I have had since I was seven years old and which I was almost too embarrassed to ask him to sign for me. During a book-signing break in the dubbing suite – for I soon realised that there were about twenty editions of *Life on Air* for him to sign – the great man spoke to me. He asked if I had 'got into the book-writing business' myself. I said no and then paused. I wanted to tell him about my wish to write a book about the pedigree industry but was worried in case he was a big fan of it. Anyway, after a few, long seconds I said, 'Well, I would like to write one about the pedigree industry.' He looked up from my book he was signing and said, 'You mean to tear it apart?', 'Yes,' I said. He paused and looked back to his work and said, 'You go for it, girl'. And that was the end of that. My mind was made up. I would get on and finish my book.

I hope Sir David doesn't mind me telling that story and I hope you don't mind me telling mine. Some of you will not like what I have to say but many of you will, I hope, benefit from it. More importantly, I hope with all my heart that animals will do so too.

The first agent I approached about this book about four years ago rejected it outright. She felt that it 'wasn't what my fans from *Vets in Practice* would be expecting'. I have had a few others tell me the same. One man very kindly pointed out that James Herriot wrote lots of book and 'he didn't sound bitter in those'. I tried not to rise to the patronising nature of this comment and said my farewells, thanked him politely for his time and walked away.

The point is that, as I hope you will see, the television shows you a fraction of me and a fraction of what is going on every day in my life, the profession and the world of pets. If you want to read fluffy tales about being a vet then I suggest you look elsewhere. I've heard that James Herriot is a very good read but if you want to know the truth about cats and dogs then read on.

Introduction: Why Is This Book for You?

On 10th July 1996 I stood in front of the president of the Royal College of Veterinary Surgeons with sixty three of my class mates and declared an oath. This declaration not only sealed my admission to the Royal College, it symbolised what I had been working towards my whole life and I deeply meant and believed what I said. The final sentence of that oath reads as follows:

'I further promise that I will pursue the work of my profession with uprightness of conduct and that my *constant endeavour will be to ensure the welfare of animals committed to my care.*'

I have strived to do this every day since then but have experienced a slow and inexorable disillusionment that has taken me through the whole spectrum of emotions from anger to bitterness to depression.

The reasons for my feelings are the main driving force behind writing this book. You, as the pet-loving public, have a right to know the facts. It is only then that the many caring vets such as myself may be able to once again truly enjoy our work and you will be able to make the right, informed choices about the animals you let into your lives.

I hope that by writing this book, and with your help, we can start to change things for the better. I have felt at times that there is nothing that can be done because it is all too big. The thing is that if we all try to work towards the same goal it is possible.

Do you want to be a vet? The many 'fluffy' animal programmes, including *Vets in Practice*, that have been a feature of our television schedules since the days of *All Creatures Great and Small* are, by their very nature, somewhat misleading. Don't get me wrong, being a vet can be a wonderful and fulfilling career. What you have to realise is that these programmes can never show the *reality* of the job. After all, who wants to watch the routine and mundane parts of any job time and again? Naturally, only the exciting and unusual cases will be shown. *Vets in Practice* and therefore I have spurred on another whole generation of people to go into this most revered of professions. If you are one of these people I want you to make the *right* decision about becoming a vet. I will give you an insight into the application process, the competition and what you can expect from your years at university. I will tell you about how wonderful the job is but I will also try and give you an insight into the other side of the job, the side you rarely, if ever, see until it may be too late. I will also try to give you some ideas about finding the right vet for your pet.

Most of all I want to stop seeing and treating diseases and deformities that we have artificially bred into our animals just because we want them to look a certain way. This should *not* be the 'norm'. The 'devolution', as I call it, of so many of our long-standing breeds of dogs and cats has gone on for too long, and although the powers that be tell us that they are addressing the problems it is up to you as the consumers of these manufactured beasts to exert your power and make these changes happen faster and as comprehensively as possible. It may be a long road but all the time there is no awareness of these things then what hope do we have? Nothing will ever change if no one ever tries.

I think it will be best if I start at the beginning so that you and I can fully understand the whole story and how I came to be the person I am now. Many people have said that, having seen me on television, they trust me and what I have to say. I am truly flattered by such remarks. I hope you will see as you read that this book had to be written. You have been misled for too long and the time has come for you to know the truth. I have reached a stage where I feel I can no longer do my job – one which I have strived my whole life to carry out – if I continue to ignore what is going on.

Everything in this book is based on the knowledge and experiences of myself, my close colleagues and my clients. As such, everything I'm about to tell you is true. For reasons that will become obvious later, I have to say here that these are my own personal opinions and DO NOT necessarily reflect the opinions or views of the veterinary profession.

Shall we begin?

PART ONE

REALISING THE DREAM

The Road to Vet School

For as long as I can remember I have wanted to be a vet. I have taken part in numerous interviews since I became the 'celebrity' that I am now. Interviewers often ask if I've always wanted to do it or what made me want to do it. The simple answer is yes, I always have, and I can't be sure what made me want to. I know that as a child I watched every animal programme I could lay my eyes on and wanted every thing I was ever given to be animal-related. It really is a question of chicken or egg. Did I do these things because I wanted to work with animals or did programmes like *All Creatures Great and Small* make me want to be a vet? I don't know but there is another possible explanation. As some of you may know from various articles that have been written about me, I was not exactly in proportion when I was born.

Judging by photographs of my head as a child I imagine that ears that big combined with placental fluids and wrinkles would be enough to make even the most doting parents wince. For my biological father it clearly *was* too much: the deep trauma caused by constantly looking at me for six months caused him to pack his bags and leave. In fact, so deeply scarred was he that he felt it necessary to move to Australia, presumably to be absolutely sure he would not accidentally bump into me in the street and have to relive the horror.

Why is it that puppies and kittens that are waiting to grow into various body parts are considered cute and adorable but children awaiting the same fate have to go to school? Surely there is enough evidence of psychological scarring to make this against the law by now. There should be a law that states that unless you are perfect in every way you should have government-funded home tuition until you *are* perfect or have left home and really should be able to stand on your own two feet anyway.

How I have rued the day that Walt-bloody-Disney ever dreamed up the cute elephant with the enormous ears! Was he indeed a great man, a visionary and a magician of the cartoon world? Or was he in fact a complete and utter bastard who ruined thousands of children's formative years and destroyed their fragile self-confidence because they were haunted by the cry of 'Dumbo' wherever they went? Surely there were enough analogies for evil primary-aged children to latch onto, such as cars with doors open or the FA Cup, without him having to create an entire character *based* on the physical deformity.

So you see, I have often wondered, and occasionally been asked, if my affinity for animals arose because I was picked on at school. Perhaps I liked animals because they couldn't articulate any crass remarks about my appearance even if they thought them. Who knows? I've talked to my husband, Mark, about this. He is of the opinion that everyone gets picked on at school about one thing or another. He moved around a lot as a kid because his dad was in the navy. Every time he went to a new school he sounded different to everyone else, so he got picked on for the ridiculous fact that he didn't have a regional accent or didn't know the colloquial term for his plimsoles!

It seems to me that a lot of confident people were bullied in one way or another. There was nothing I could do about my ears, although I contemplated many methods of rectifying them including super glue and that old *Blue Peter* favourite, double-sided sticky tape! Sooner or later you just realise that it doesn't matter. It took me years but eventually I came to think it ridiculous that I should worry about someone not liking me because *my ears stuck out.* This is one of the great things about growing up.

Although I was obsessed with all kinds of animals when I was a youngster, horses were my favourites. I desperately wanted one. I even entered competitions to try to win them. Let me put it this way, I had the entire collection of *Black Stallion* books and watched *Champion the Wonder Horse* religiously. The theme tune to *Black Beauty* still sends a shiver down my spine.

Enough said. Anyway one year we went to the New Forest for our holiday. Mum and Dad had told me about all the ponies and I was bursting with excitement. I made a solemn promise before we went that I was going to stroke every pony I saw. This was a mistake. Everything was going well until we decided to go for a walk. Halfway across a field I trotted off to stroke a lovely grey

4

pony I had clapped my eyes on. It is probably worth pointing out that when I was young I was as thin as a twig. My granddad affectionately called me 'Bony Em' after the pop group. So there I was stroking the pony. I must have done something wrong because without warning it turned round and bit me in the chest. I actually left the floor for a couple of seconds, suspended by what would, in later years, become my left breast. I still wonder to this day if this is the reason my left one is larger. You know, like the *Just So* story about how the elephant got its trunk.

Needless to say this partial maiming did not deter me. It would become the first in a long line of minor savagings by various animals I have tried to help over the years. An occupational hazard, one might call it.

It soon became completely apparent to me that the horse was never going to arrive in the long-dreamed of horsebox with the bow on it. I was lucky enough as a child to have grandparents who seemed to be better off than we were. As a result my grandma and granddad started paying for me to have horse-riding lessons. I loved this and have now ridden for many years, although today I just don't have the time to devote to a horse of my own.

With the horse being a thing of dreams, my next option was to start the long process of coaxing my already stretched parents into having a pet. You can imagine how pleased they were about this. I should point out that I am a freak in our family. Not only because of the ears (and some fairly alarming feet) but also because I am the only one in the family that likes animals. Don't get me wrong, the others would not torture puppies or anything like that but they have never really got why they mean so much to me.

The first to arrive was Mogsy. Dad had taken us over to see grandma and granddad one day and stopped at a farm shop on the way to get some apples. We waited in the car and Dad eventually emerged with a large cardboard box. We thought he had probably bought too many apples if he needed a box to carry them in but didn't mention it. He was grinning madly as he put the box in the back seat and started driving home. We knew something was up and peaked in to see a tiny, black and white bundle of a kitten. I was ecstatic. Mogsy spent the first three days of his time with us hidden under a wicker chair in the front room. He was petrified, probably mostly by me, as I was almost constantly half-wedged under the same chair trying to make friends. The poor cat was probably scarred for life.

It wasn't long before the next stray turned up. Some good friends of Mum and Dad had a yellow Labrador called Daisy. They had to move due to circumstances beyond their control and could not take her with them. I awoke one morning to the screams of Joanna, my older sister, who did not share my passion for animals. She had gone downstairs and fled at top speed back into the room saying there was a massive dog at the bottom of the stairs. I was out of bed like a shot. This was the best news I could get. I desperately wanted a dog. Daisy and I became best friends. I would help look after her and spent most of my time mauling her around, as small children do with their pets.

We had had her about six months when one morning I came downstairs to find Daisy wasn't in her usual place. I assumed she was in the garden and went out to find her. As I came back in, Mum was in the kitchen and told me Dad wanted to talk to me in the front room. I went in there and Dad was looking really bad. I remember his words because I played them over in my head for months and months afterwards. He said, 'Last night I took Daisy out for a run and she got run over and killed.' To say I was devastated is an understatement. She was my entire life. I was totally devoted to her. She was running with Dad on a quiet road up at the army barracks and started playing with another dog. A car came round the corner too fast and killed both the dogs. I was completely distraught. I had never lost anything or anyone I had loved until then. I am not exaggerating when I say I cried myself to sleep *every single* night for several months. I couldn't stop thinking about her and the accident. I even wrote to *Jim'll Fix It* to ask if I could have a statue of her made like the one *Blue Peter* had of Petra. I remember crying as I wrote the letter and then drew round a fallen tear and annotated it so they would be in no doubt about how upset I was! Surprisingly they never got back to me.

With four kids in a two-bedroom house the last thing Mum and Dad needed was another dog. Then a puppy came our way. One of the teachers at school had a Jack Russell that had recently had a litter and needed homes for them. I begged Mum to have a look at them, knowing that if she did she would not be able to say no. Sure enough Smudge joined the family … briefly. Smudge was a very cute puppy but turned out to be totally unsuitable. He was very snappy and had an insatiable appetite for chewing. The problem was that he didn't really mind if he was chewing the furniture or the toddlers so very soon he found himself back at the teacher's house and I found myself without a friend again.

By the time I turned eleven I had just about given up hope of getting another dog. On our birthdays we were not allowed parties because we couldn't really afford it, so we had a tradition of 'birthday treats'. We were allowed to invite one friend and we could choose the treat. This usually involved birthday tea and a trip to the ice-skating rink or the cinema. On this particular birthday we had been out in the day and had had the obligatory birthday tea with cake and candles. We were about to settle down to watch a film when Dad suddenly got up and put his coat on and told us we were going out in the car. We were a little bemused but off we went. He stopped at a house and went to the door leaving us in the car. We watched him talking to the woman for a while and he returned to the car. He put the light on and looked at a list in his hand and spilled the beans. He had a list of unwanted dogs from the RSPCA and had gone to see about a litter of Labrador puppies but they had all gone. He said he didn't think the next one on the list was really what we wanted but all the same we could go and have a look.

We drove to another house and we all trooped in, and that's when my friendship with Penny began. She was a six-month-old collie-cross. She came up to us and immediately rolled over on her back. I wanted her immediately. The woman who owned her had a small child and said Penny wasn't house-trained and she couldn't have the baby crawling around in 'it'.

I don't remember much about the film that night because all I wanted to do was play with Penny. I have a perfect mental picture of the whole night from the minute Dad got up to go out and I hope it never leaves me. It is my experiences with Penny that have helped me be a better vet. Having pets of my own has shown me things that vet school could never teach me in a million years. Once you have owned, loved and had your heart broken by a pet you can then truly empathise with a client who is going through those same things.

Universal University Rejection

As I've said, I knew from early on that I wanted to be a vet. I worked extremely hard at school but was not one of the most academically gifted pupils. What I did have was a drive that was all-consuming. I knew I had no choice but to get the right grades in the right subjects. My whole life was focused on this goal. Fortunately I had superb teachers for both the subjects I found hardest, namely physics and chemistry. I have the nightmare of entropy diagrams etched into my soul!

When I went through the process of applying to university there was really only one choice and that was to put all five universities offering the veterinary course on the form. I say five because I was not bright enough for Cambridge and I didn't apply to Dublin because I could only put five down. Nowadays the application process has changed for courses such as veterinary medicine, human medicine and dentistry, where the number of applicants is so high. UCAS now states that students can only pick a maximum of four out of a possible six choices for any one of these subjects. You can, however, pick, for example, four vet courses and two medicine, you just can't have all six choices for the same course. In fact if you try and sneak them on and pretend you didn't know they won't even process your application.

I'm sure that there are thousands of you who have applied to vet school and failed. This is because it has one of the highest applicant-to-place ratios of any course. Most people when they hear you are a vet will come out with all the stock phrases like, 'Oh, you must really love animals', 'It takes seven years to be a vet, doesn't it?' (no, it takes five), 'It's harder to be a vet than a doctor, isn't it?' (no, it's just harder to get in because there are so few places available that they have to put the grades up to reduce the number of applicants) and 'It must be hard because the animals can't tell you what's wrong' (working from first principles is usually

8

much less misleading than I imagine a lot of the things doctors get told by their patients!). My point is that it seems as if everyone knows how incredibly hard it is to get a place.

Like many other students I waited eagerly to hear from the universities. I didn't care which one I went to as long as I went. My predicted A-level grades were three Bs. As it turned out this wasn't good enough. Over the next few weeks I had straight rejections from Liverpool, Glasgow, Edinburgh and Bristol. My only glimmer of hope came in the shape of an interview at London. My Dad took me up there and waited for me. I came out a shadow of my former self. It was absolutely awful. I'm sure I deserved the pasting I got and was probably horribly underprepared but the memory is not a good one. It feels in my mind like I was a tiny speck on a chair in front of five giants whose job it was to make me realise how inconsequential I was. Needless to say, shortly after that I got a rejection letter from them too.

I will never forget the day Mum took me to school to collect my A-level results. As I had no place at university secured, we arrived early so I could try clearing if the grades *were* OK. We walked into the office and Mr Wood, one of my favourite teachers, was sorting out reams of paper. He looked over and looked at me in a very non-committal way. I asked if the results had come in and he said yes and seemed to be giving nothing away. My intestines were trying to desperately fight their way out of my mouth. It seemed as if my entire future was resting on the small piece of paper with my name on it.

I heard myself ask him what my results were and he told me very calmly, and with a small smile on his face that I will never forget, that I had two As and a B. It was at this point that I remember thinking he must be joking and that it was not funny to do that to someone. He handed me the piece of paper and I still couldn't believe it. Mum gave me a massive hug, we both started crying and she was telling me how proud she was. It's a moment that will stay with me for ever. I had worked so hard for those grades and I knew I had earned them. I was ecstatic.

Unfortunately they didn't really help in the short term because there were no places to be had for love or money. I was resolute that I was still going to be a vet so I decided to have a year off and get some experience and try to make myself a more attractive proposition to the universities.

Work Experience

The comprehensive school in the village of Hoo in Kent that I attended from the age of thirteen to eighteen was fantastic. I had originally gone to an all-girls grammar school after my eleven-plus but due to a house move had changed schools. It turned out that the results for my A-level year were far better than the grammar school achieved and many aspects of the teaching and facilities were superior. However, the careers adviser knew less than I did about what was necessary to get into vet school. What he should have told me, and what I am telling you, is that work experience is *absolutely essential* to your application. It is one of the few ways in which you can distinguish yourself from the hoards of other people trying to get on the course. The sheer numbers of people achieving the grades means you need something extra. *You* may know how desperate you are to be a vet but as well as wowing the universities with all your amazing extra-curricular activities and interests you also have to make yourself stand out from the crowd.

I would also recommend you do work experience from as early an age as possible. Do whatever you can – work at a kennels, work on farms and at riding stables, work in pet shops and, most importantly, work at your local vets. It can be quite hard to get a placement but persevere because it will do you no end of good in the long run. I had only done a week of work experience at the local PDSA during my school time and I'm sure this affected my application. As a result I had to really go for it in my year off.

I got a voluntary placement at a practice in Maidstone and spent three months working there. I wrote notes on everything I did and typed up case studies the same as I would at university. I absolutely loved my time there. I was happy to muck in with all the crap (quite literally) and made thousands of cups of tea. The vets who worked there were very varied. Most were fantastic and some were tyrants, and we all learned to live with the outbursts from the more highly strung among them.

I remember an absolute classic day when one of the scarier vets was in a particularly foul mood. A dog had been brought in bleeding from a cut paw. There was a trail of blood from the front door to the prep room. He came storming out the back and shouted that it looked like a bloody butcher's shop out the front and why hadn't it been mopped yet? There was a scared silence in which all the nurses and I went pale with fear and grabbed mops and buckets to sort it out. As I mopped my way through the practice the vet in question was still storming about and huffing a lot. He was dressed for theatre and had surgical clogs on. He came firing across the patch of floor I had just finished mopping and did the most farcical, Monty-Pythonesque fall I have ever had the pleasure to witness. In full view of all the people he enjoyed intimidating he completely left the floor. Both legs went up parallel to his body, and he seemed to hang in mid-air for several seconds as everyone grimaced and waited for the inevitable result. He came down to earth with an enormous crash and landed right on his backside. You could have heard a pin drop. About three nurses and myself suddenly had very important jobs to do out in the kennel room. We practically ran out there and burst into explosive, side-splitting laughter. The sort that is all the better because you know you shouldn't really be laughing. It was glorious.

When I had finished my time there I pestered as many of the vets as I could for references to send to universities and then went to do some farm work. I spent a month working on farms during lambing and calving and got proof of it to send as well. I started applying as early as possible and sent my case studies and references.

This time round I was offered interviews at Glasgow, Edinburgh and Bristol. I was again rejected outright from London and Liverpool. The Edinburgh interview was first. I was very nervous but felt I had shown I had the dedication and I already had the grades from the first time round. The interview seemed to go quite well but I dared not hope.

It was about a week later that I couldn't bear it any more. I rang and asked the receptionist if she could tell me how far my application had gone. She disappeared to have a look for me and I don't think I breathed once during her absence. She returned and said, as if it was the most everyday thing in the world, that she was pleased to tell me they were offering me an unconditional place. This still makes me get goose bumps when I think about it. It was a defining moment for me. I knew with certainty for the first time that I *was* going to be a vet. The thing I had strived my whole life for and I had done it. I was standing on the bottom of the stairs at home when I found out. I just about managed to say thank you and hang up before my legs gave way.

It was shortly after this that I went for my interview at Bristol. I would have gone anywhere to do the course but I really wanted to go to Bristol, mainly because it was slightly nearer than Scotland but still far away enough to make the break from home. It did not go well.

We left in plenty of time the day of the interview. My mood soon declined as we got onto the M4. It was completely fog-bound and the traffic was crawling at a snail's pace. We stopped at some services to ring the university to tell them I would be late. I was frantic; this would surely look very bad. It got worse.

I arrived about two hours late, and as I was called into the little room the man commented on the fact I was late. I was crushed, they hadn't passed on the message, he hated me already. I did the interview, which flew by and was only about ten minutes long. I really couldn't tell if I'd said the right things or not.

Well, as you've probably guessed, I was offered an unconditional place and was once again over the moon. I cancelled my interview at Glasgow and accepted the offer at Bristol. I had a few months left and got the opportunity to go to Canada for three months to stay with my brother-in-law's family. I got a pub job to get some money together and went to Canada.

University

Many people will tell you many different things about university. The things that stand out for me are these: they were some of the best times I've had so far, it helped me leave home gradually and in a fairly controlled way, and it helped me form my own opinions. This last point I found out quickly. We all have opinions from a young age but they are usually closely linked to our parents' or those of the people we consider our role models. The thing is that often we haven't heard all sides. When you go to university you are thrust into a mix of people from every walk of life. You really learn a lot from this and I think it is one of the best reasons to go. You learn how to live with other people, and you learn that there are *some* people that you simply *can't* live with. You also learn how to live with yourself.

When you first arrive at university it can be quite hard to break the ice with the people on your course. The vets at Bristol have overcome this with something called the freshers' treasure hunt. This has the effect of lifting you quite a long way above the ice and then throwing you through it really hard. It takes place the first weekend you arrive. You are instructed to go to the Union and not to wear anything you ever want to wear again. You are also asked to take the grimmest things you can think of to use as missiles. The most pleasant of these were usually eggs; I won't go into the less pleasant ones.

Once at the Union you are bundled into cars and vans either belonging to older students or hired for the occasion. You are then driven at very high speed round Bristol and the outlying villages gathering the things specified on the list and trying to work out the cryptic clues to each place you have go. The objects varied, but examples were a bale of straw (we were in a Mini the year I did it) and a hubcap from a competing vehicle. The checkpoints that are led to by the clues are actually scrumpy stations where

13

you are obliged to down a cup of the ropiest cider the older vets can find. The thing that makes the whole thing more fun is that if you see another competitor at any point you have to try to bomb them with your missiles. The hunt culminates on the Mendips where you are forced to play drinking games with more of the same cider. The first person to vomit is proudly named as your year's representative, a selection procedure that could probably be put to good use in the political arena!

As you can imagine, once you have seen your fellow students encrusted in egg, flour, cider and vomit the barriers are pretty much broken down. I distinctly remember standing in the shower back in halls, leaning against the wall, unable to move and hoping that the dried egg in my right ear would somehow wash itself out because I, quite frankly, was not up to the job.

There are many people who think that five years is an awfully long time to be at university. I was extremely grateful for it. During the first three years of the course we got to know a lot of people that were leaving after three. These years went so quickly that it really seemed like it wasn't enough. We had the bonus of another two years. They really were some of the best times of my life.

I could regale you with numerous, sordid tales but that is another story. The point is that I was learning the trade for which I had prepared my whole life and there was a part of me that couldn't wait for it be over so that I could get stuck in. A fairly common feeling on the course is that you just don't get to maul enough animals until the last two years. I suspect this is a fact for which the animals are incredibly and rightfully grateful.

When I was at university I worked much better under pressure (this is still true today). Seen in one way this makes me sound great. I imagine myself as a character from *ER* performing amazing feats of concentration while all hell breaks loose around me. What it in fact means is that I am a lazy git who finds it incredibly difficult to get motivated until the very last minute.

This manifested itself as cramming for exams like crazy when the levels of adrenalin in my system had risen so high that I would find myself waking up at three in the morning in a mad panic. I would wake up sweating, and inwardly screaming, 'I've left it too late, I can't possibly pass, I don't know enough!' You get the gist. I would then get up and work during the night. I remember things much better if I do them at night. I am an owl and will always be. I have come to the conclusion that I ideally need a job that starts at 11 a.m. and ends at 9 p.m. I could then stay up until midnight or one or two as I do now but without feeling like a zombie the next day. Consequently, my parents spent every end of year with a nervous, stressed, gibbering wreck in their house because I couldn't bear to stay around my fellow students at exam time.

Many of my friends revised by making copious revision notes. In one case my friend Tara would literally copy her notes over and over again because this was how she absorbed the information best. I tried this but gradually came to recognise how my brain works. I remember things by picturing the words on the page. The layout of the letters, the colour of the ink. Even down to what side of a piece of paper the information is on. In the end the only way I could learn was by staring at my notes for long periods of time. The problem with this is that it is very easy for the mind to wander onto more interesting things. The vet course is a huge amount of mostly dull, and seemingly irrelevant, information so it takes a lot of concentration not to start thinking about the pub or the fact that the sun is shining, or the fact that you would rather chew your arms off than read another list of pharmaceuticals or the temperature and humidity at which a duck egg needs to be kept in order for it to hatch.

Eventually, by the fourth year I had perfected the technique of putting really loud music on and reading my notes out in a loud voice so that my feeble mind would have to stay on the job in hand. As you can imagine, this is a fairly antisocial way to revise and I'm sure my friends were glad that I always went home for study leave. The selfish truth is that it wasn't for their benefit, it was for mine. Being the sort of person who never really knew whether they had done enough, I found it utterly intolerable to be suddenly surrounded by the bunch of know-it-alls that my friends seemed to turn into in my head at exam time.

I suddenly saw their smiles of hello as smug grins as I pictured their enormous brains overflowing with all the facts that had so far escaped me. Every night we would go to the local pub to get away from the books for last orders but our usual rule of no shop talk would soon evaporate. There would be about half a conversation about something normal and then some bastard would have to mention something they had learnt about the packaging of meat in Public Health that day. I would sit there and think, 'Oh God, I don't know that.' I would suddenly be transformed into Joey from *Friends* as all my mates talked fluent vet and all I could do was nod along and smile knowingly while I screamed inside.

So off to Kent I would go. My parents were saints and silently tolerated the outbursts of stress and hysteria that always followed me home.

Despite the stress I had hundreds of great times and I absolutely loved my time at university. I was very lucky in that I was in a year full of people that had very much the same attitudes as me to having a good time. Lots of people say that when you are there you have the time to enjoy yourself but not the money and when you leave you have the money but no time. This was certainly true for me, and so I decided to borrow enough to have a good time and have thankfully now repaid the enormous debt that I left with.

The Final Year

By the time I reached the final year I estimate that I had spent roughly seventeen years trying to get to that point. That is no meagre statistic. My entire life had been about being a vet. All the hours of pretending to inject and bandage toys, the hours and days and heartache put into the application process, the work experience, the rejections, the A-levels; all of it was about this year and my final exams. I had had a wail of a time, but I had also worked extremely hard and had been through a lot of very cathartic moments.

The final year was full of peaks of success and anticipation and troughs of utter despair and depression. My life depended on me being able to remember the contents of about twelve full lever-arch files and countless handouts and textbooks. It is estimated that the average vet student forgets more facts than are taught in a normal three-year course. You are required to assimilate one fact every second for the whole five years. Well, that is how many facts are presented to you. Of course, it is impossible to know everything. You should leave with a basic knowledge of every subject and be able to apply what you have learnt to a diagnostic process. At the time, though, it seemed like an impossible mountain to climb.

In the final year we also started doing proper veterinary work. By this I mean that we were actually allowed *to touch animals*! I love surgery now and it is one of the most satisfying parts of my job, but I can tell you that when you are first asked to pick up a scalpel and cut into someone's pet it is pretty scary to say the least! Our first forays into the world of surgery were somewhat worsened by possibly the most unforgiving learning atmosphere. There was a certain member of staff deeply involved with teaching us the art of the knife who seemed to have made it his mission to destroy students' confidence. I feel I cannot speak too badly of him because he has since passed away, but I feel there are probably a lot of vets out there that still shy away from the theatre because of the crushing words and actions of one man.

All this aside, I loved the final year and, if you didn't act like a complete gimp, the staff were very decent. There was another member of staff called Avril. I hope she won't mind me naming her. She was head of anaesthesiology and was another name that would strike fear into most students, particularly female ones. Now I started out resenting this. I thought she should be a bit fairer and try to encourage people more. It is very difficult to recall anything when you are terrified and I felt it was detrimental to our final stages. I was once asked by her to calculate a drug dose in my head having been told the weight of the dog and the percentage of the solution required. I didn't have a clue. My maths has always been a weak point and I stood there like a feeble-minded bimbo. She made me look a fool but I guess in hindsight I deserved it in a way. I made sure after that that if I went into one of her surgeries I bloody well knew what I was talking about and she was always extremely fair to me and was very praising when you did something worthy of it.

On the whole, the staff at Langford were absolutely brilliant. Peter Holt, Dan Holden, Alistair and Frances Barr, John Huxley, Geoff Lane, to name but a few, were stars.

And so it was that we careered towards our finals with astonishing speed. We worked our rotations of things like surgery, small-animal medicine, equine and so on. We became more tired by the day and the nerves started to show. Bags got bigger and frowns deeper. Conversation became more hushed and the library started to fill up. I never went to the library because I have a problem with them. I find it impossible to relax in such a highly charged atmosphere. It's like you can hear all the internal workings of people's overstretched and undernourished brains. It drives me crazy. I get an irresistible urge to stand up and suddenly shout at the top of my voice just to ease the tension. Places that are that quiet but full of people are completely unnatural. In fact, I didn't even know where the main university library *was* until the third year.

We started to get a feel for what being a vet would actually be like. Obviously I knew from watching *All Creatures Great and Small* that every day would be spent saving lives and generally being the most respected member of the community. Let me tell you something, James Herriot has a lot to answer for (as I suppose do I, having made *Vets in Practice* for seven years and playing my role in misleading another entire generation).

I remember one week in particular. During the holidays the students had to take it in turns to look after all the animals at Langford. There were three of us at a time starting at noon on a Saturday and finishing at noon the following weekend. This may not sound like much of a big deal but I can tell you a lot of it is in the lap of the gods or, if you are an atheist like me, it's just plain luck.

Looking after the animals at Langford consists of a lot of what all vet students learn to hate and that is the TPR. This stands for temperature, pulse and respiration. These are the three key measurements of how alive an animal is that must be recorded whenever an animal is 'checked'. In most cases this is done twice a day but in the case of intensive care can be hourly. In a normal week in term time you have to do this in a group of four for one component of the place such as the horses *or* the cats *or* the dogs but not all of them.

So we gaily arrived at noon on the Saturday and the previous clerks told us what was in and reported that the week was not as bad as we had been led to believe. Or at least that *their* week wasn't that bad. At about four o'clock we received the worst possible news: a surgical colic was on its way. Colic in horses is not uncommon and is really a general way of saying they have belly ache for one reason or another. Many cases are not too severe and are caused by spasms of the guts. Some colics, on the other hand, are caused by blockages, tumours, obstructions or twisted guts and the like. These will almost always require surgery and are always emergencies because horses can quickly go into shock and die in these cases.

This announcement was bad news for a number of reasons. First, it was coming from a fair distance so wouldn't reach us for some time; second, colic surgery is usually very long and, third, colic surgery is fraught with danger and very stressful. Most importantly for us, surgical colics require hourly post-op checks twenty-four hours a day for at least two days.

I must admit I was quite excited about the prospect nonetheless because they are good to see and be involved in. Anyway, I think we actually got the beast on the table by about 7 p.m. and started into the two or three-hour operation. About an hour and a half in Frank Taylor, the clinical dean, disappeared and returned some twenty minutes later. Frank Taylor is another of Langford's stars and is the sort of man that you constantly want to hug because he's so nice to everyone. Unfortunately for us, he sauntered cheerfully into the room and happily announced that another surgical colic was on the way. A lot of tired oh-you're-such-a-joker type laughter ensued and gradually petered out as we realised he wasn't joking.

I think we started the second one at about midnight and then stayed up all night checking them. The following day our third surgical colic arrived and our fate was sealed, or should I say our week was totally and irredeemably screwed. Three surgical colics in two days is a record for Langford, and oh how lucky we felt to be part of it. TPRs on the other in-patients became a glance through a kennel door to ascertain if the animal was alive, three numbers similar to the last ones recorded were duly written down and we dragged ourselves to the next case.

By the following Saturday, and another surgical colic on the Friday, I felt a mixture of emotions. The overwhelming one was that of sheer and indescribable exhaustion but there was also pride in the fact that we were the ones who'd had the most hideous week possible. We knew without a doubt that the story of that week would resound around the Golden Lion for years to come. At least we felt like real vets. We'd spent the week saving lives and rushing round full of our own self-importance. It was great. I was finally doing it.

Finals

I think I will have great difficulty conveying exactly what finals are like. The format has changed somewhat now to take the pressure off a bit but when we went through it was basically a test of everything. There was one week of written exams, followed by a few days to revise everything you cocked up in the written papers, then the vivas. These are oral exams and are incredibly nerve-wracking and potentially very humiliating. They usually consist of one of your lecturers plus an external examiner to make sure it is all fair and above board. There is enormous speculation every year about what the nature of the questions is likely to be and also rumours abound about the various external examiners and how much of a bastard so and so is in an oral exam.

The hell for me was that I had come back from study leave feeling just about OK about how much I knew only to be immediately immersed into a group of people who might as well have been talking a foreign language for all I knew. Then there was the torment of past papers. Some of my friends had very diligently got hold of copies to get an idea of what to expect. I'll tell you what they made me expect. I took one look at one paper and knew that I was simultaneously going to be sick, crap myself and start crying. I would then get completely and utterly shafted from every side, having ruined all my parents' expectations and years of them paying for me to be at university because I was a lazy, good-for-nothing alcoholic. You can imagine my mental state throughout my finals was not that balanced, but then I think the only people *not* in that state were Steve and Alison, basically because their lives did not revolve around the worship of various types of fermented fruits and plants.

The timetable for the exams was published and it was nothing short of a nightmare. The exams were all in the morning over about six days. The problem with this is that you revise for the next subject and that is all your head holds. Everything else you've learnt in the last five years gets temporarily shunted into a siding somewhere between your arse and your elbow and it is very difficult to retrieve it. So you go and do a three-hour exam about, let's say, small-animal surgery. You then want to curl up in a ball or run into the Mendips and beat yourself with a thorny branch for all the time you've wasted. *But* instead of this you have to steel yourself, force yourself to trudge home and start trying to extract everything you know about farm-animal medicine from a place that doesn't exist in any anatomy text book.

This goes on until you finally reach the end of the written exams. You also have to put up with brief moments with friends where they start dissecting the paper and telling everyone what they put for what questions. This is the most basic form of torture for a useless wastrel like me. I would resist the urge to run away with my hands over my bloody Dumbo ears shouting 'la la la la la' at the top of my voice so as not to hear the answers I was so sure I had got wrong.

By the time the oral exams arrive the local pharmacies for miles around have run out of Pro Plus and all the local shops are rationing the sale of coffee. The village is now populated with shrivelled beings that resemble people you used to know or think you used to know. They look forty years older and can barely manage a grunt in greeting to you. They guard the folders they carry as if their lives depend on them. And in a way I suppose they did.

One of the downsides of having world-class lecturers is that they all tend to be very absorbed in the subject they teach. This is fine and is perfectly understandable but it does get a bit much when someone gives you a 400-page handout on ophthalmology. Now I know eyes are important but when you've got to assimilate 400 million other facts that people think you should know it is not very useful. My solution to this was to pretend the subject didn't exist. I kind of blanked it out like someone suffering from post-traumatic stress does to the initiating incident. This worked very well indeed for the written papers because I simply didn't answer the ophthalmology questions or wrote particularly bad, please-fail-me-at-once answers. However, my plan came unstuck when I got to my vivas.

In one of my vivas, a very nice man called Stuart Carmichael was the external examiner. Now I knew he was an orthopaedic specialist, so those pesky eyes seemed a distant worry. He mentioned

Jack Russell terriers and I brightened. He asked me if presented with such a dog what sort of things I might expect it to get wrong with it. 'Aha!' I thought. Small dogs get luxating patellae (slipping knee caps) and this is right up Stuart's alley. I proudly announced the fact and he said that, yes, I was right. The problem was that that was not enough for him. 'Anything else?' he asked. Panic set in. Surely I wasn't expected to know two conditions a breed might have unless it was a German shepherd dog which gets every condition known to veterinary science. He could see I was floundering and sinking deeper and deeper into an abyss so, bless him, he tried to help me out. 'Perhaps something with their eyes?' he prompted. The cavern underneath me widened and I started to slip towards the hell that was re-sits.

He tried again. Rarely have I seen such a valiant effort to save someone's career. The guy deserves a medal. As with many things, I will liken it to a scene from a film. I apologise to those of you who have not seen *Pretty Woman*, but there is a scene at the hotel where the manager confronts Julia Roberts (who plays a hooker) about her undesirable presence at the hotel and tries to give her every opportunity to redeem herself. He suggests that she is perhaps a relative of Richard Gere, perhaps his niece. The penny finally drops and the situation is smoothed over, to everyone's relief. There are few times in my life when one could compare me to Julia Roberts, but this was one such time. Stuart doggedly continued to try and get me to say that Jack Russells get lens luxation. After quite a few awkward silences we finally arrived at the diagnosis and then started the uphill struggle to try and drag out of me that, yes, it needed treatment and, yes, it was fairly simple and, no, it probably wouldn't make that much difference to its eyesight. We reached the end and I think I was close to breaking him, but he was made of stronger stuff than I and he triumphed.

There is a kind of hysteria that comes over students at exam time. It is the fine line between holding it together and losing it completely. I walked this line with the skill of a tight-rope walker for five years and it is testament to what the human body can endure. I have a perfect photograph that sums this up taken the night before our written exams started. We set up my camera to take a photo of Jon, Andy, Hannah and me and the emotions are etched perfectly on our strange and varied expressions. It is a photo that I will treasure for a lifetime.

I will also never forget the moment outside our first exam when the lovely Frank Taylor was giving us a pep talk. He was saying that even if you don't know the answer just try and write something, even if it was only your name. It was quite a humorous thing to say but it was met with a massively undeserved group belly laugh befitting of one of the world's funniest comedians. This is a sign of the hysteria that constantly bubbled close to the surface during this time. Laugh or you won't just cry; you'll collapse in a blubbering mass of organs and skin on the floor.

Somehow we survived. I still don't know how. I was probably averaging about four hours sleep a night for about a month and putting my brain through the most vigorous workout it had ever had. The amazing thing is that your body just keeps going and going. It's like it knows that the end is in sight and if it can just hold on you will reward it with sleep and beer. By the end of finals you feel as if your body has drawn the line. It is saying, 'OK, enough is enough, you have to stop now.' The fact is that it would have kept going for longer but when the adrenalin stops pumping everything just shuts down. You think you were lucky because you only just made it but it is nature's way of surviving. Those incredible chemicals that used to make us stand and fight or run for our lives now course through the same vessels but for different reasons. It is survival all the same.

Realising the Dream

Me and a very proud Mum at graduation.

© Emma Milne

I think the day we finished our exams and got our results will stay with me until I die. I can honestly say that it was (probably sadly) the greatest, most incredible day of my life so far. I'm sure everyone who has had a child is wryly smiling to themselves and saying to their partner, 'Ah, how naive she is!' But seeing as I haven't had *that* particular experience yet, I will make do with this one.

It was a boiling hot and sunny day and we were sweating in more ways than one about our vivas. Mine finished at lunchtime and I had the afternoon to kill until the provisional list of results came out. This is produced incredibly quickly because they already have a rough idea who has passed and who hasn't after the written exams. Basically, if your name's on the list you're a veterinary surgeon and if it isn't your life disintegrates in front of your eyes and all hope of enjoying the summer vanishes in an instant.

So, what should I do for the next few hours? It doesn't take a genius to realise that those of us who had finished headed straight for the pub. We chose the Langford Inn because of its close proximity to the vet school and the fact that it sold a large variety of alcohol. It is one of those screamingly British country pubs with all manner of dead and stuffed animals adorning the walls, but at a time like that I was willing to put that thought aside.

We supped a few ales and the grins were as wide as the ocean and the anticipation was almost tangible. Joe and I headed back to Langford after a while to play football of all things. Joe had just done an incredible sliding tackle straight into my left shin when the ball was deflected off at speed towards the buildings. While I lay writhing in agony on the floor and clutching my almost certainly broken leg Joe went off to get the ball. He returned quite a while later and simply said, 'Guess what?' The words 'I don't know, it is that you've broken my leg, you bastard?' drifted through my mind but all I managed was, 'What?' He said, 'We're both vets,' and then stared at me in a strange unnerving way. I sat there stunned while the information sank in. There is half of you that is celebrating and cheering and mentally doing laps of honour round the field and the other half that's thinking 'That's a pretty bloody mean joke.'

There were a few seconds where we just kind of stared at each other and then he finally, after what seemed like an eternity, managed to gather himself to say that when he had gone to retrieve the ball he had seen the secretary entering the building to pin up the list. Naturally the pessimist in me had to go and look for myself. Even though I knew I had passed, it just didn't seem real and I still had an incredible feeling of fear as I approached the board as if I had no idea what to expect. The list was in alphabetical order and it took a while for my shrivelled and overworked brain first to remember my surname and second remember where it came in the alphabet. I remember standing staring at the list and an uncontrollable smile started to appear on my face. This gradually grew until I resembled the Cheshire cat from *Alice in Wonderland* and after a while I felt like I had lockjaw. I think that smile stayed with me for about four days.

That moment that I knew without question that I had achieved my lifetime's goal was truly indescribable. I know people talk about drug-related highs but I'm sure the natural chemicals that were floating around me would beat any of those hands down. I was awash with the most complete and totally deep-seated contentment. At that moment I didn't have a single care in the world. All my life's work up to that point was suddenly crystallised into a dazzling whole-body fulfilment. I don't even begin to have the vocabulary or the imagination to fully describe how I felt, but I think you get the gist that it was pretty great.

There isn't much else to say about it really. We left for our graduation holiday about a week later and that was the best holiday I've ever had. Sixty-five of us went and took over an apartment block in Turkey. A small group of us met a fantastic boat captain called Eyup (his name gave us great amusement). We spent nearly the whole two weeks, including several nights, aboard the *Mislou*, his boat. I don't think I have ever relaxed like I did on that holiday. It was like weights had been lifted off all of us and everyone was just happy to be alive. We roasted ourselves for two weeks and became intimately acquainted with a local drink called raki. If you've never had this, don't try it. It is like drinking a cross between Pernod and paint-stripper.

Aboard the *Mislou* with Eyup and crew.
© Emma Milne

Eyup realised one day that we all really liked the song 'Hotel California' by The Eagles, and especially the line, 'So I called up my captain, please bring me my wine,' and so he decided that whenever we were on his boat he would just play that song over and over. That song will forever take me back to the top deck of the *Mislou*: my skin is dark brown, there is a smile on my face and the water is so clear it looks too shallow to swim in. I am surrounded by my friends and there is nothing life can throw at me that I will not be able to deal with.

It's strange how misleading happiness can be. As it turned out the next few years were to be a very gradual but steady slide into uncertainty, cynicism and unhappiness with my chosen path.

'Make Me Famous'

Alice and Sharon at Glastonbury Festival.
© Emma Milne

The phrase 'make me famous' is one my very good friend Sharon shouted one sunny, glorious afternoon at the Glastonbury Festival while ridiculing my early forays into fame and celebrity. We had gone with my sister Alice and were having a fine time away from our respective lives and other halves. Sharon worked for the BBC at the time and we had met when she was a researcher on *Vets in Practice*. Now she had the mixed pleasure of being charged with filming Alice and me at the festival. The fact that she got any usable footage out of it at all is testament to her directing skill! We had quickly become friends and shared many 'television' moments. Sharon is a great one for mocking herself mercilessly and also anyone else who is within distance. We had often joked about the whole fame thing and she constantly abused and mocked

29

me at every opportunity. She loved to mock our fake celebrity because she, like all those who know me properly off screen, realise it is all a bit of a farce.

As many of you will know, the television cameras started following us around when we were but quivering, final-year wrecks. I remember hearing a wild rumour that BBC Bristol were thinking about making a series about us in our final year. Most of us were terribly excited, some were appalled at the idea and some positively gagging for stardom. A woman called Sarah arrived and spent a while talking to various members of the year trying to ascertain who the 'characters' were. There were some obvious choices like Steve because he came from an astounding family of vets and because he is very outgoing and confident. There was Fiona who was a mature student and had done another degree prior to the vet course. Trude was an obvious candidate too because she had luscious locks and a killer Scandinavian accent. I also think it is fair to say that there was an inkling that she might be borderline for the exams and this too was of interest. Personally, I was excited to be filmed but disappointed not to be included in the first series, *Vets School*. I say I wasn't included but there is definitely a shot of my shoes in one episode, a glimpse of me outside exams and a brief shot of Steve, Joe and me doing a spectacular, synchronised back flip in Turkey.

The cameras quickly became a thing of normality. It was no different to everyday life eventually. I still did find it a little embarrassing to turn up, say, at the RSPCA neutering clinic with a film crew and it did sometimes raise some hackles, probably because people assume you are going to start lording it about like a rock star. I hope I have never been guilty of this. I have to say on this tack that I have had the excellent good fortune to meet quite a few 'celebrities' since being on the tele and the vast majority of them have been great. However, there are the odd few, as anyone will tell you, who are frankly rude and need pulling out of their own arse. Being famous to any degree does not make you special and it most certainly does not make it acceptable to treat other people with contempt or a lack of respect.

The fact is that we all saw it as a bit of fun. No one expected it to carry on past Bristol. It was our chance at our fifteen seconds of fame and we jumped at it.

When I first qualified I worked at the practice in Maidstone for the summer as a locum. (It had been my foster practice all through

30

university.) I was living with my parents before moving to Exmoor to start my first job. It was at home that the phone call came. The BBC had been overwhelmed by the popularity of the first series and they were thinking of making a follow-up called *Vets in Practice*. They asked if I would consider being filmed for part of it. Well, after my crushing disappointment at my removal from the original I snatched their hand off. Again, I thought it would be a one-off series.

Seven years and eleven series later I still get recognised, including in many foreign countries where the programme has been shown. It was a massive success. The fact that our personal lives were shown too gave us this extra dimension. People actually started to feel like they knew us. It really is an odd sensation. It must be very weird for actors in soaps where the public see them as their character. At least for us we were just being ourselves.

I have been asked time and again if I regret agreeing to the first and subsequent shows and my answer always has been and always will be a resounding 'no'. You see, I see it as a fantastic and rare opportunity. I have experienced things that I could never hope to experience as a 'normal' person. I suppose a lot of people who wish for celebrity are hankering after the glamorous side of it and the great parties. One of my best ever nights was going to the National Television Awards. We were nominated for best documentary in 1999 and Joe, Hannah, Trude and I were asked to go to the show. I was also asked whether, were we actually to win, I would accept the award. I was ecstatic at the offer having assumed Trude would be the obvious choice.

We were collected from our hotel in a flashy saloon car and driven to the Albert Hall. I have never known anything like it in my life. It was like something out of *Notting Hill*. The door was opened and we were let out in front of the building. There were hoards of the public on one side shouting your name and asking for autographs and banks of photographers on the other side shouting for you to look this way and that for photos. I was completely blown away by it. What on earth had I done to deserve that kind of attention? It is a truly bizarre concept that I could have that much adoration simply because I had let people see how I live my life. I find it even stranger now with programmes like *Big Brother* to see how simply being on the television can turn you into a superstar.

31

We stood in front of the photographers (several of whom thought I was Ulrika Jonsson, not for the first time in my life!) and soaked up our superstardom. In truth we were completely out of our celebrity depth. We knew we didn't belong there as much as everyone else did. We spent the entire evening agape with whoever it was we had just brushed shoulders with. I was trying to be cool as if I went to that kind of place every day and, I imagine, completely failing. It amazes me that people that are properly famous can even stay sane. I know a lot of them don't, but living in the public eye is an odd place to be.

As well as people getting the wrong end of the stick about you as a person, when you are relatively well known there is also a staggering misconception about the supposed wealth that comes along with it. I never really thought about it before but it seems that everyone thinks that if you have appeared on television you must be a millionaire. I have been asked numerous times how much we were paid, and many people with slightly more subtly and tact have made comments like 'You must have no money worries!' Of course there are numerous superstars that we hear about all the time that are on the rich list but the majority of people in the lower echelons of television are not numbered among the mega-rich. For the purposes of *Vets in Practice* the BBC were onto a money-saving winner because we were just ordinary folk and were not classed as presenters. For the first year we were paid £500, and this rose over the seven years to the unearthly sum of £4,000 for the final year. This didn't bother me because I had not agreed to the filming for the money. It was just for fun, as they say.

I was asked a couple of years ago to return to my old school and give a speech for prize-giving evening and present the students with their tokens or books. I was very flattered to be asked and the evening went really well. After the event and during the wine and nibbles several of the students asked me to autograph their books for them. I was more than happy to oblige but couldn't help thinking that a few years down the road they might regret asking when nobody had ever heard of me! During the melee I was signing a book for a young woman and her proud dad was standing close by and chatting about television work. He made a veiled remark about how loaded I must be and, being a little weary of it by then, I simply told him the exact figures. He was obviously astounded and then asked me what else I did to survive. His embarrassed daughter looked up from her book and said, 'Dad! She's a vet.' With the same stunned look on his face he uttered the immortal line, 'What, you actually are a vet? Not just for the series?' I'm not sure to this day how many other people were under the same illusion that we were just employed to be vets by the BBC. For those of you that may still be confused, we went to work every day just like normal vets and the cameras came along every now and then to eavesdrop on our lives.

I think we have been luckier than most celebrities because we tasted the good side of it briefly but we are 'z-list' in reality and can lead normal lives. When I say 'we', I have to excuse Steve who has risen through the celebrity alphabet in style and is now a superb presenter – lucky bugger!

The glamorous side of it is a very occasional bonus, but for me it has meant much more than that. Being a little obsessed with animals, as you may have gathered by now, the television has opened doors that have meant that I have been able to reach more animals and people than I ever would as a normal practising vet. I have had numerous letters from people and positive comments about how much admiration people have for me. This is an incredible position to be in. Don't get me wrong, I'm not blowing smoke up my own ass and I've had plenty of letters from those who have disagreed with me. The fact is that all the 'campaigns' I have been on since I became a little famous have been so satisfying for someone who feels as strongly as I do about animal care and welfare. I'm not an extremist, I'm not even a vegetarian, but I am informed and I believe in what I say. Many people have come to trust me and that is why I can no longer keep this book from you. There are massive welfare issues at stake here that most of us never consider.

While I was being filmed for *Vets in Practice* it became a bit of a joke, as it has among many of my family and friends, that I carry a soapbox under one arm almost continuously. Few things give my family more pleasure than sitting down to dinner, waiting for a pause in the conversation and then saying something like, 'So, anyway, what *is* wrong with hunting?' They absolutely know that, even though I am completely convinced that they are trying to wind me up, I just won't be able to resist it.

I did try to get some of these points across during filming; after all, they were issues that I felt deserved air time. Unfortunately it wasn't that kind of show and fluffy bunnies and young vets' misfortunes were much more appealing to the powers that be.

I don't want to knock the show. I absolutely loved being involved in it and it was excellent entertainment for the millions of people who became regular fans. Without it I wouldn't be doing many of the things I am. Even when things went wrong for Joe and me I didn't doubt I had made the right decision. The people who worked on the programme with us, in my experience, were friendly, fun, caring and enormously sensitive to us as 'subject matter'. I have made some great friends in the process and had some amazing experiences and some fantastic belly laughs.

The programme ended up becoming a bit of an institution. We won the award by the way and, for those of you who've wondered, we didn't know we'd won until they read out the result!

Another question I often get asked is 'What's it like having your job filmed?' This is the weird thing now that it is all over. Until the programme ended I had never had a job where I wasn't being filmed. When the cameras left after their final day I was incredibly

The 'dream team' BBC crew of Don, Debbie and Max in Egypt.

© Emma Milne

sad. I had known these people for years. They had become like a family that showed up at work and made it more fun. The other thing was that we had always shared everything with all of you. I had this strange sensation that, well, what's the point if no one's going to see it. It had become so ingrained in us that we just accepted it. If I planned a big night out or a reunion with friends or a birthday came around or any interesting cases came in, it was a knee-jerk reaction to see if anyone wanted to film it. As I say this I know how bizarre it sounds, but that was my whole life for seven years.

Vets in Practice, no matter how 'fluffy' and soft it was, was pure entertainment. I realise wholeheartedly that I am privileged to have been involved.

The Dream Starts to Become the Nightmare

In hindsight there were signs that all was not well with the world of animals when I was at university. Now I see that I did not recognise them for what they were because I was blinded by the blinkers that I had on about becoming a vet and saving animals. I also just learnt the facts and accepted that that was the way things were. Now I realise that the mountain I have to climb is that you lot out there, through no fault of your own, are also blinded and accepting of too many things. It's not because you are stupid or unwilling to look further but it is because you have been shielded from the truth for too long. You are relying on the people in the know to inform you and you have been sorely let down on a number of scores.

You need the facts so that you can make your decisions armed with those facts. You see it's not until this is properly in the public domain that I can continue my work. I can't stop boring the life out of my family with dinner-time rants about the latest case. If I just carry on plodding along doing my daily job and keep all this to myself I will die a very troubled and unfulfilled person.

It is only fair to warn you again before we start that this is going to upset a lot of people. However, I know in my heart of hearts that they will be in the minority and if my plan works then I will help a lot of people and their pets. So I'm sorry if you're a bulldog fancier or the owner of the Pekinese that won Crufts but I'm afraid nothing is going to stop me saying my piece. It is just my opinion and if you don't like it, don't write whining letters to me slagging me off, get off your arse and write your own bloody book. Actually don't bother, because part of the reason this goes on and so many people are duped into buying unhealthy, disadvantaged animals is partly because there are already so many books extolling all the virtues of these animals.

I hope I've given you the odd chuckle so far, but it's only fair to warn you that it is all about to get very negative and cynical. I'm sure I will be accused of making sweeping generalisations – I am bound to in order to get my point across. You must accept that I am about to tell you the worst examples of everything in order to make that point. Don't blindly take my word for it – do some research – but have faith in the fact that nothing I am about to tell you is a lie. They are all facts that I have been privy to in the last fifteen years. The fact that it has been my lifelong goal to be a vet and I am now on the verge of throwing in the towel must count for something. In fact, the powers that be may feel that I no longer have the right to be a vet after this, and so be it if that is the case. The decision will be out of my hands.

As I said at the start, I hope that by writing this book, and with your help, we can start to change things for the better. I have felt at times that there is nothing that can be done because it is all too big. The thing is that if we all try to work towards the same goal it is possible. I want our pets to be cared for better, I want owners to give more thought to their animals' lives, I want to you to make the *right* decision about becoming a vet, and most of all I want to stop seeing and treating diseases that we have artificially bred into our animals just because we want them to look a certain way. This should *not* be the 'norm'.

As you will see, there are many things about my job that I absolutely adore, but I do think that being a vet is very different to what many people perceive. I want to detail this for two reasons. One is to give those of you contemplating making it your career an understanding of what it might actually be like so that you can make an informed decision. The other is to show how incredibly stressful the job can be and I hope that if you can see and understand what we have to do then you may be able to grasp some of our shortcomings and difficulties.

PART TWO

THE TRUTH ABOUT BEING A VET

Under Pressure: The Stresses of Being a Vet

Before we begin I should point out that I am talking about small animal general practice here. It is about eight years since I did any farm work so I can't really comment. What I will say is that I really enjoyed my time doing it and it was definitely what my mum would call 'character-building'. The coming mini rant about on-duty time really doesn't apply to farm work; when a farmer calls you out you just go because you can be sure he definitely needs you – farmers don't waste time and money on vets they don't need!

There are many different stresses to be considered in our noble profession. The major ones will follow but first let's look at an aspect that is frequently overlooked by prospective vets: PEOPLE. Invariably and rather obviously most prospective vets are desperate to work with animals. In most general practice jobs, however, you must realise that most animals come accompanied by a person or sometimes several people. Talking to and dealing with clients can be the best bit of your day but it can also be your worst nightmare.

In the coming pages it is going to seem like I am really berating clients and having a go at them. I *must* say at this point that annoying clients are by far and away the minority, but anyone who deals with the public will know there are bound to be some bad ones. I am lucky enough over the years to have met some wonderful people and would count a lot of clients as close friends. All the clichés about 'there's nout as queer as folk' and so on pale into insignificance when you mix animals into the equation. Owning animals induces a type of madness in some and this mix of devotion and insanity manifests itself in some very odd ways. As many a vet will say: 'I still love working with animals, but I just wish they wouldn't bring their owners with them!'

I have thought long and hard about the best way to describe the reality of a vet's life and dealing with awkward clients and the conclusion I've come to is that I will give you what I call a preparation plan. By this I mean a kind of trial run. I estimate that you will need to carry out the plan for a minimum of three months in order to get a real taste of what it's all about. There will be certain elements that you cannot re-create such as surgery but I will try to find a close approximation.

The first thing you need to do for the plan is to pick a topic that you are not particularly interested in. Research one small aspect of this topic and write yourself a ten-minute speech about it. You must then commit this to memory to the point where it starts to infiltrate your dreams at night.

The next step is to repeat this speech to at least two people every day, word for word, throughout the entire preparation period. This should give you some idea of what it is like to spend every summer explaining to someone why their dog won't stop itching and is gradually trying to eat its own body from the feet up. (It soon becomes very wearisome when you see animals that have all the classic symptoms of flea-allergy dermatitis but whose owners insist that their pet has had 'everything there is for fleas'. It usually takes approximately three seconds to ascertain that the dog has had everything there is for fleas that you can buy from a supermarket but never a veterinary product that has actually been proven in the last twenty years to kill fleas.)

For your next step you need to make a list of about ten people that irritate you so much that you would rather boil your own head than spend a second in their company. You *have* to be as mean to yourself as possible here. I don't want to find out that you secretly included some of your best mates and ended up becoming a vet and got fed up with it and then blame my preparation plan. Once the list is compiled you must randomly invite them over to your house for a cup of tea and a chat throughout the month. You must also ask each of them to pick a time that is convenient only to them and to ring you whenever they feel like it to ask you something totally mundane. To be completely realistic this should preferably be at your busiest time of day. You must also pick one day in the month when you arrange for all the people on the list to visit you in quick succession, preferably when your day seemed to be going very well and you were actually feeling quite good about yourself.

This should introduce you to the 'heartsinkers'. I learned this phrase after reading Nick Hornby's book *How to Be Good*, which is written from the point of view of a female doctor. The phrase is one I immediately adopted because of the striking clarity and succinctness of it. It is fairly self-explanatory and simply means that it is the kind of client whose name on the daylist or voice on the phone makes your heart sink. They are the clients, happily the minority, that can, with one word, reach into your chest and grasp your heart so tight that your blood pressure goes through the roof and you need ten deep breaths to get yourself under control before you die of an aneurysm.

Next we will try to simulate your time on duty. Now don't get carried away here and don't think for one minute that you are going to be re-enacting scenes from *ER*, riding a trolley through the surgery while giving a recumbent corgi CPR and screaming things like, 'I need a CBC, 'lytes and a chem. 7.' And *never* assume that you will ever be excused for uttering the word 'stat'.

To break yourself into it gently, first pick two nights a week as designated nights and one weekend during the month that includes Friday night to Monday morning. On these nights you also need to designate the place we will be calling your surgery. It should be a minimum of ten minutes' drive from your house and a maximum of twenty. During your on-duty time you must not partake of any alcoholic drinks whatsoever and you must not go anywhere that is further than twenty minutes from your 'surgery'. You must also not go anywhere that precludes you from talking on the phone, such as pubs rammed full of drunk people having a much better time than you and making too much noise for you to hear your phone.

On your first night on duty have a shower or decide to cook your partner a nice meal. Just as you have shampooed your hair or just as the potatoes are coming to the boil, stop everything. Get dressed, switch off the oven and drive to your surgery. Sit there for between thirty and ninety minutes and then go home again. Try to salvage what was left of your night.

Do this a few times and then add the element of surprise by asking one of the people on your heartsink list to ring you randomly at some point while you are on duty. For maximum effect this should be at about 4 a.m. When they ring, leave the room so as not to disturb your partner and go and stand naked in the bathroom talking to them for about ten minutes. When the conversation is finished, get in your car, drive to your surgery, sit there for an hour and then go home again. Make sure that you get up at the normal time the next day because contrary to popular belief a night on duty does not guarantee a day off the next day.

Once you feel you are confident you can handle yourself, go for the weekend. Preferably this should be a really nice, sunny weekend. It should be the kind of weekend that makes you immediately want to make the most of the two days of English summer and go and have a pub lunch and sit in the garden and see a few of your mates. We'll be kind and say that Friday night is very quiet. You speak to a heartsinker at 9 p.m. but they don't require your assistance; they just wanted to make an appointment for tomorrow and assumed you would be sitting at the surgery all night waiting for their call.

On Saturday morning make sure that you get up at normal working time and then make sure that you do not let a single ray of sunshine touch your body until at least one in the afternoon. Pick a chore that you have been trying to put off for ages like pulling out all your own teeth with a rusty pair of pliers and spend the morning doing it. On Saturday afternoon drive round where you live and glare enviously at all the people sitting in pub gardens and laughing with their friends over a nice, cold pint. Go to the surgery at least twice between the hours of one and seven in the evening, preferably leaving home the second time just after you have arrived back.

Leave again at eleven thirty and drive to the house of the farthest person on your list and spend an hour there to simulate a house visit. Perhaps they have had a little too much to drink to come to the surgery and they haven't noticed the problem with their animal until the pubs chucked out. Go to bed at about one and set your alarm for eight on Sunday morning and go to the surgery again. Repeat this a few times throughout Sunday and make sure that one of the visits is just as you're about to eat Sunday lunch with your parents.

This should give you a fair idea of how much of a pain being on duty can be. What it cannot prepare you for are incidents such as these:

A man finds a stray dog. It is uninjured. He has rung the RSPCA, the dog warden, the police and four other veterinary surgeries before you but has been told to go elsewhere or encountered an answerphone on each occasion. You then drive to the surgery, scan the dog, find it has no microchip and put it in a kennel in the surgery where it proceeds to destroy the kennel and howl all night, keeping the neighbours awake.

A couple ring you at about six in the evening one Sunday and say they are concerned their dog may have something lodged in its throat. In the background you can hear the dog retching and coughing as if it is about to expire. You immediately agree to go straight to the surgery and see the dog. On questioning the couple reveal that the dog started this behaviour yesterday morning but they had a wedding to go to so they waited until they got back thirty-six hours later to call you.

You receive a call at seven thirty in the morning from a woman whose cat is very weak and cannot stand. By the time you see it, it is practically dead. While you are trying to convey the urgency of the situation to the woman and extract the cat from her for some emergency medical attention she tells you that she has 'sat up *all* night with the cat'. This turns out not to have done the cat too many favours because it dies shortly after arrival. It is three years old.

Sunday evening you are summoned to the surgery by a man with a very sick cat. He had been away and the cat has been cared for by a friend. It is very elderly and had stopped eating and drinking and had become very weak. You think, 'Oh well, he isn't to blame. He's been away and has returned to find his lovely cat not looking too good.' You casually ask the man in the course of the consultation while examining the poor beast where he had been and so on. You get talking and sympathetically ask if he has returned just that day to find the cat so ill. 'Oh no,' he says, 'I got back on Wednesday but I've been very busy since then.'

A client rings you at four in the morning to discuss their bill and is somewhat surprised to find out that you were in bed and not at the surgery.

You are rung at three in the morning by a very concerned family that report that their dog is sitting in the kitchen looking very worried. You have trouble keeping your mouth shut when all you want to do is shout, 'It's looking worried because the whole family is standing in the kitchen in the middle of the night staring at it!'

A client rings you at two o'clock in the morning to make an appointment for the following day.

... Anyway, you get the idea. I don't think there are any vets who resent being on duty when there is a genuine emergency. They can be extremely satisfying cases to treat and I for one would want to know that if my dogs Badger or Pan needed help there would be someone there to do it. However, it is incredible how many people abuse the situation for their own convenience. Have some respect for your vet. They work bloody hard. It is because of this minority that vets charge so much for out-of-hours calls. You finally get to the point where you have to have something to put people off doing it. I know it sounds bad but it's the harsh reality. I know of one vet that had got so fed up with it that he used to make a note to himself in the daybook when he'd seen such owners that said 'HIW' – 'Hit in the Wallet'. You will find that a little bit of sleep deprivation does some strange things!

Now I think we are getting a taste of what it is all about. There are some aspects of the job that I can never fully explain unless you live them. Being a vet is like being a GP, a hospital and an accident-and-emergency unit all rolled into one. For this reason your day can never be planned. You can try but you will invariably fail. My day consists of morning surgery followed by operating followed by evening surgery. If I was a GP I would just have the surgeries, a surgeon would just have the operations and the A&E would just have the emergencies.

The trouble is that you will have your day planned out and ordered and then a dog, through no fault of its own, will manage to find the only piece of glass in a four-mile radius and will endeavour to slice one of its pads open in such spectacular style that their owner thinks its leg is about fall off or it will bleed to death. They quite rightly arrive unannounced and you have to start shuffling.

There's a saying: 'Patience is a virtue.' It is arguably not one of my strongest points and I fear I may be running out of it altogether. However, it is certainly one that you will need if you are to survive the jungle that is veterinary medicine. You must also never underestimate the ability of clients to listen intently to every word you say and then go home and recreate a completely different set of instructions in their heads.

There are a lot of veterinary 'urban myths'. I will recount a couple, although in all honesty I cannot vouch for their authenticity. There is the one about the client who had the dog with a bad ear. They were given some tablets and some drops for the ears. When the vet saw them a week later for the check-up he asked how they had been getting along. The client replied that all was going well to start with. The dog was taking the drops very nicely in his food but after about four days they simply couldn't fit any more tablets in his ear!

There is also the story of the client that was given a whole pot of tablets for an ongoing condition. When asked if medicating the dog was going well they reported that the majority of the tablets were going down very well but they were having some problems with the big, cylindrical ones. The vet realised that they had been feeding the dog the silica capsules that are put in the pot to soak up the moisture that could damage the medication. Apocryphal or not, these stories are perfect illustrations of how communication can break down and things have the potential to go disastrously wrong.

Having dealt with clients we'll look at the other stresses that can get to you. I see these as physical, mental and emotional. Vets have one of the highest suicide rates of any profession. Obviously this may be because we have the access to the drugs and know how to use them, so we may succeed where others fail. (At least when we do something we do it properly!)

The physical stress is probably the easiest to deal with because you become accustomed to it very quickly. Besides the obvious energy exerted doing large-animal work, it is surprisingly hard to simply stand up all day long as is the case with small animals. God only knows how many miles I walk in a day but by the time I get home my legs have usually had enough. I am particularly looking forward to the varicose veins I am bound to develop by the time I am forty-five.

The mental stress I would put next on my list. (Some vets may place it at the top but for someone who gets ridiculously attached to the animals like me the emotional stress can be much harder.) When you are at school you have lessons of about half an hour to forty minutes. University lectures are about fifty minutes. There is a good reason for this and it is because the average attention span of a human is no more than an hour. As a vet you can expect, on the vast majority of days, to have to concentrate fully for about ten hours and that's before you start a night on duty. Yesterday I worked at the surgery from eight thirty until seven, got called out at nine for half an hour, got called back out at eleven, operated for over an hour, got home at two thirty, went to bed at three and got called again at eight this morning. This doesn't do a lot for your mental agility.

The demands on your time are enormous, and even if you are not consulting or operating, there are usually about five people expecting phone calls or there are lab results to be interpreted or paperwork to do. It can be incredibly exhausting. It is always amusing in a sadistic way to observe a group of vets at a social occasion. A house phone rings and there is a definite little shock wave that goes through every one. Some will check their phones or pat their pockets without being conscious of it. The phone becomes your enemy. I have been in numerous supermarkets or other shops and had the same feeling of dread when the phone rings. I'm sure it is psychologically damaging. I get 'told off' by many of my friends because I am so bad at keeping in touch. The fact is that I talk all day long every single day. I am sick to death of my own voice by the time I get home and I have used up all my listening reserves. My husband, Mark, and I sit at home and cower away from the damn thing like frightened rabbits. So please forgive me if I haven't phoned you for a chat in the last six months – I'm just telephonophobic!

As a vet, for every minute of your day, someone will want a piece of you for something. There will always be a 'to do list' that will never quite get done and sometimes it will all seem a bit too much. In previous relationships I have managed to invoke innumerable rows because of the steam I let off for the first ten minutes after I get through the door. It's not until the Shiraz has started to unwind the knots that I can relax and calm down. You can easily appear to be 'taking your day out' on a companion but in truth you are just resetting your sanity to make it possible to get through the following day. Invariably you will awaken an hour after you've dozed off and remember that you forgot to phone a client or put some clinical text on a record. Have you ever noticed how many people in my profession are constantly covered with self-inflicted graffiti? There are days when I have felt like a large, walking Post-it note!

A good friend of mine is called Julie. She is probably the best nurse I have worked with and we met when I was working at an extremely busy practice. It got to the point where she actually bought me a spiral-bound notebook and some string and tied it

48

round my neck. This was the only way she could ensure I got the messages because I never even had time to remember to go and look in the message book that lurked by the front desk. I would be happily examining a dog or looking at an X-ray and she would bustle into the room and half strangle me while she wrote the latest summons in the book. She has always been very effective at getting vets to work as hard as she does!

The advances in medicine and surgery are rapid and the requirements to stay abreast of these are paramount. We also live in an increasingly litigious society. While I do not for a moment suggest that veterinary wrongs should be hidden or ignored it is a fact that the fear of being sued is a new stress facing vets, on top of the awful fear of making a mistake.

For the last couple of years I have been involved with the Society of Practising Veterinary Surgeons (SPVS) annual conference for final year students. Besides the lectures they run tutorial groups to give students a chance to voice their fears and concerns and as a society they offer loads of support for all concerned. My tutor group this year said that their biggest worry after their finals was being struck off. They were frankly terrified that they will have worked their whole lives to achieve a goal and it will be taken away from them. This struck me as incredibly sad.

We are a profession but we are also human. It is easy when everything is at your fingertips to find it hard to deal with the times when you realise you are not superhuman after all. A recent survey found that many vets also found it very hard to deal with the fact that they could not always do what they knew to be best for the animals because of financial constraints or, more often, time constraints. You need to be realistic if you enter the profession. I'm not saying accept being substandard but realise there will always be limitations of some kind or another. I also realise that conversely some of these limitations may be perceived by clients as you not doing your job properly and we are back into the cycle of concern about complaints. Hopefully this book will help parties from both sides have some idea of what the other is dealing with. For this reason I have also included the chapter on finding the right vet if you are unhappy for some reason.

Finally you have to deal with the emotional stress. There are quite a few people that have levelled at me that I shouldn't be a vet because I get too attached. This does cause some heartache for me but I strongly believe that if I lost that attachment I wouldn't be a very good vet at all. There are numerous occasions that I have broken down with clients over the death or euthanasia of their pet. I often wonder whether this is very useful. Surely I should be there to be a rock of support for these people at one of the most difficult times people encounter. I can't help it. I have tried not to cry but as a child just the theme music to *Lassie* would set me off so I'm on a bit of a hiding to nothing. I like to hope that the clients see me as caring and not about as much use in a crisis as a kick in the crotch.

Emotional stress is not an easy part of the job to convey and I suspect you'll probably have a good idea whether you are the sort of person who might be greatly affected by it or not. The following two chapters will hopefully give you an insight into what I find one of the most challenging aspects of the job.

Losing Penny

Penny in her later years.
© Emma Milne

I think this as good a place as any to finish telling you about Penny. Partly because it fits my timeline but also because when I lost her it was a pivotal moment in not just my life but my veterinary career. It wasn't until this time that I fully came to understand what people go through when they lose their pets. I know now that part of the reason I get so upset at the time of euthanasia is because in some way it always takes me back to Penny. Even after many years it still brings me to tears.

I don't think I was very good to Penny. I was young when we got her and as many children do I wanted a pet but I didn't want all the boring jobs that went along with it. In my teenage years I didn't really walk her as much as I should have and I didn't want to stroke her every time she came to me. I think all this guilt has

51

hopefully made me a better owner to Pan and Badger. Having said all that, I absolutely loved Penny. She was always my dog and even after I left home whenever I came back she was always there for me. She saw me through all the years at school, all my moods and depression at not getting to university and eventually the joy of finding a place and then my graduation.

She was a scruffy mutt but she could clear a six-foot wall in her prime and she always forgave me my shortcomings. When it was time for me to return to university she would sense my imminent departure and would lay in her bed and sulk and refuse to come to me unless I called her several times. If she could she would hold out until I went and lay down next to her basket and gave her a cuddle to say sorry. She always waited at the bottom of the stairs for me and she always lay under my legs when I sat on the sofa, just like Badger does now. She was my constant best friend and I will never forget her.

As she aged I convinced myself that she was going to live for ever. When she got to about fourteen she really started to age quickly and became very stiff from arthritis. She started to go a bit senile and doddery but nothing she or we couldn't cope with. This went on and on and her decline was so gradual that we could never really decide that she was bad enough to have her put down. I started to worry about it because I was now fully trained and it was on my mind.

Eventually she was starting to have problems getting up and down and we decided as a family that I would go home the following weekend and I would put her to sleep. Many people find it hard to believe that I chose to do it but I felt that she knew and trusted me and it was the least I could do for her after all she had done for me. I was incredibly upset at the prospect and it was constantly on my mind after the decision was made. We never made it to that weekend.

I received a phone call at work from Dad on the Wednesday to say that she had gone off her legs completely and couldn't stand up. I broke down at work and said that I would drive to Kent after evening surgery. I told Dad that I wanted to do it as soon as I got there and not have polite chit chat because I couldn't bear it. I asked my boss at the time if I could take the things I needed from the surgery and if we could rearrange morning surgery so I could drive back the following day. He said that was OK but asked that I be back by lunchtime to operate and do evening surgery. At the time I thought this was a little insensitive as I was effectively about to kill the dog I had had for sixteen years. Nevertheless I agreed to be back.

The drive to Kent was awful and the rest of the evening I cannot even begin to describe. When we arrived Penny had managed to get up and was pottering around the way she always did. I found that despite my resolution to get on with it I just couldn't. We all glossed over it and had dinner and talked about everyday things while we all tried to pretend we weren't going to do what we were about to do. After dinner I couldn't take it any more and I broke down again and said, 'Can we just do it?' It was at this point that Rebecca, the youngest of us, became inconsolable and ran upstairs crying.

I now found myself in a very strange situation. I was the grieving owner, distraught at the thought of losing my pet, but I was also the professional that had to go upstairs and try to explain to Rebecca that it was for the best for Penny and that we weren't murdering her. The truth was that I felt exactly the same. It was at that point that I realised with startling clarity that I had made every decision about her whole life. I decided when she ate, played, slept and went for a walk. And now I was deciding when she died. I felt exactly like a murderer.

We sat Penny in the kitchen and she had that look on her face as if she couldn't understand why we were so upset all of a sudden. We all crowded round her trying to comfort her and she just sat there looking at me. Giving her that injection is the single hardest thing I have had to do in my career. She slumped gently over on one side and it was all over. There was silence in the room except for the muffled sound of self-conscious tears being shed. I can't tell you how I felt. I'm sure many of you will know.

Afterwards we sat in the living room talking and Mum got up and started clearing Penny's bowls away into a cupboard. I couldn't stand it. It was like she was removing all the evidence of her existence. I asked her to stop and she said that she just couldn't look at them but left them where they were for my sake. Strangely, about an hour later I was looking at her bed and thinking about when we would come back at the weekend. I knew I wouldn't be able to look at it without her there and ended up asking Mum to make sure it was gone by the time we came back.

The one thing I will never forgive is the reaction of my boss when I returned. I was late because of traffic and didn't get back in time to operate but was back for evening surgery. I rang en route and left a message to that effect. He was livid. The following day he took me into a small room and balled me out about the fact that I had taken a pair of scissors and he couldn't find them and he looked stupid in front of a client because of me. He went on and on and then said something I will never forget: 'I had a *really* bad day yesterday because of you!' I stood in front of him desperately trying not to give him the satisfaction of making me cry and all I wanted to do was scream: 'Well, I had a pretty fucking bad day too!' I should, in hindsight, have done so and I should have told him to stick his job where the sun doesn't shine. I should have told him what a contemptible little man he was. But I was too weak and upset and I kept my mouth shut. As a vet I believe it is *absolutely* unforgivable to make a time like that any harder than it is and this is a principle I will stand by all the time I am a vet.

My Worst Week

I am going to tell you about my worst week now and I hope you don't mind. I want to use it to illustrate the sometimes distressing nature of the job but I also want these animals to be remembered. I should point out that it was exceptionally bad and should not be seen as the norm by any means. Indeed, I hope I will *never* go through a week like it again as long as I am a vet.

My boss of the time, Alison, was away on a very rare week's holiday so I was in sole charge of the practice. This is something I do on a daily basis so it was not a problem. It did mean I was on duty almost every night because Alison usually did the same thing, through some feat of endurance that never ceases to amaze me. On the Sunday night at midnight I saw one of my favourite clients with her pug, Chaucer. Edwina and Chaucer had been coming to see me for about four years. By this point I was very fond of both of them. Chaucer was a stoic little creature. He had only one eye from a dog attack, and a permanent head tilt from a car accident prior to his rescue by Edwina. He snuffled and guffawed the way all pugs do and usually wandered into the odd cupboard door while at the surgery. He was a brilliant patient despite everything he had been through. As the years had gone by I had also removed quite a few pieces of his ageing body too!

To this day, Edwina is one of the most incredible people I have met. She is what most people would consider elderly but is one of the strongest, most awe-inspiring women I know. I must admit that I had prejudged her when we first met because she had a pug, which, although a lovely-natured dog, is one that has been deformed by years of inbreeding. As the years went by and we talked more and more I found that she is a soulmate and an incredibly principled person. She has not eaten dairy products for years because of the suffering of the calves and has osteoporosis as a result. I also found that she had always loved pugs since she was a child but

55

now only took on rescue ones and fully agreed with me about my views on what has happened to the breed over the years. She informed me in her indignant way one day that she would certainly *never* buy one. Edwina has had an amazing and rich life and has both harrowing and wonderful tales to tell. She is an inspiration and I will always be glad that I met her.

Chaucer had deteriorated a lot and we had known for some time that the end was nigh. He was in a bad way and quite a lot of pain. I gave him a combination of drugs that would make him sleepy and pain-free and told his mum that if there was no change by the next day we would have to put him to sleep.

My first job the next day was that very thing. We both knew the drugs were simply providing Edwina with the time to prepare herself for the inevitable and she brought Chaucer down early the next day before morning surgery got under way. I knew him like he was my own and I saw his owner as a real friend. One of the hardest things at times like this is the distress of the owners. Having been through it myself with Penny, I have come to realise that the way this situation is handled is *the most important* thing that I can do for my clients. Most of the time you know it is for the animal's own good but the grief that strikes the owner left with the gaping hole in their lives is unbearable. I shed my tears briefly then gathered myself for morning surgery. We had a mental day and Emma, the nurse, and I got to the end of it and consoled ourselves with the fact that the week could only get better. How wrong we were...

Tuesday morning heralded a phone call from another long-standing friend and client with a very sweet Cavalier called Henry. This woman had taken him on as a rescue dog and had spent inordinate amounts of time, energy and money ensuring that his quality of life was as good as it could be. He had countless problems spawned by genetic back-firing and needed constant attention. He was only middle-aged when his owners decided that finally enough was enough. I agreed and Emma and I went to the house to put him to sleep. Again, my tears were brief because I knew I had to return to the other animals that needed me. There was an air of disbelief as we drove back to work and a gaping silence in the car.

One of the operations for the day was to take a biopsy of a very aggressive-looking lump on Churchill's foot. Churchill was a scruffy, old boy who belonged to Caroline and Martin who run the local wildlife rescue charity we did work for. I had become close friends with them in the previous year and had become a trustee of the charity. On exploration I found that the mass involved all the deep tissues and tendons of his foot and could not be excised. We sent the sample away for analysis and Churchill went home.

On Wednesday I thankfully didn't have to end any lives but towards the end of the day we had a fax from the lab to say that Churchill had a highly aggressive and malignant tumour. His only hope, if there was no spread, was to amputate his leg. We booked the op for Thursday, with the proviso that X-rays of his chest showed no spread of the cancer. By this time I was starting to struggle. Having had day after day of bad news and having to go through all those emotions without being able to release them fully because of the pressures of work, was starting to take its toll on my sanity. I became increasingly pessimistic and said something that I fatalistically regret to this day. We ground our way to the end of Wednesday and I was in tears after telling Caroline the bad news. I sobbed at Julie, our other nurse and my very good friend, 'Now all we need is for something to happen to Elgar.'

Elgar and his owner were in the same vein of dream clients and animals. Elgar was a bear of an old black Labrador with a heart of gold and an appetite to match, partly because he was a Labrador and partly, as it turns out because he had a disease called Cushing's. We had diagnosed it earlier in the year and his medication was doing wonders. His 'mum' had happily told me that he was once more enjoying his walks. He was also on heart medication and tablets to stop his legs getting stiff from the arthritis that is so common in older dogs. We only saw him for routine check-ups and there was absolutely no reason to think he would have a problem.

Thursday dawned and Churchill arrived for his tests. Caroline and Martin knew that if the tumour had spread there was nothing we could do. Needless to say in that week from hell the X-rays showed that his lungs were riddled with cancer from his leg. I was starting to lose it by this time and had to ring Caroline to say that, as we had agreed, we would not let him wake up from the anaesthetic. We were both in tears on the phone and she told me to go ahead and put him to sleep. They came to pick him up and it was excruciating. I knew I couldn't take much more.

Friday seemed to come and go remarkably without incident. It was the first night that week that I was not on duty as Alison had organised a locum to cover. At the end of surgery Julie and I decided the only option was to go for a beer. We went to the local and sat outside and pondered on what a dreadful week it had been. She left to go home after about an hour, and Jamie – my boyfriend at the time – and I sat and finished our drinks. We were just about to leave when my mobile rang. I wasn't too bothered because the phones had been diverted to the locum. The last name in the world I wanted to see was flashing on the screen. You see, Elgar's mum and I had become close too and we had been to see them socially and she had my mobile number. She could have just been calling for a chat or to see when we would next be meeting up for dinner but somehow I just knew it wasn't going to be and I felt like my guts were being wrenched out.

I almost couldn't bring myself to answer the phone and stared at it in disbelief with my words of Wednesday night ringing in my head. She, bless her, started off by apologising for calling me when she knew I wasn't on duty but no one else had ever really dealt with Elgar in the past three years. She told me that he had snaffled the cat's food as usual and suddenly collapsed. She couldn't rouse him and he had no strength at all. I told her to bring him straight down, a journey that would take about half an hour.

We started to walk back to the car and I couldn't do it any more. Elgar was the final straw. My body started shaking and the tears came. They weren't just for him, they were all the tears I'd saved all week for Chaucer and Henry and Churchill and all the other animal friends I'd lost over the years and all the wonderful clients I had come to treasure.

We got to the house above the surgery where Alison lives and we were staying while she was away. By now the floodgates were well and truly open and I was close to full-blown hysterical wailing and sobbing. Jamie kept telling me I had to hold on a bit longer. 'Hold on for Margaret,' he kept saying. He phoned Emma and asked her to come in to give me a hand.

I sat and cried and chain-smoked and shook as I desperately tried to regain my composure. Margaret arrived just as I had managed to compose myself but it was obvious I had been crying. I walked out to the car and we just hugged in the car park. She opened the back door and Elgar was lying on the back seat. He

58

didn't have the strength to raise his head. A quick look at his swollen abdomen and his pale flesh told me he was almost certainly bleeding internally. We stretchered him into the surgery and a needle inserted into his abdomen produced whole, dark, red blood. A ruptured splenic tumour was the most likely cause and I gave Margaret the option of trying to remove it. She agreed we should do whatever we could and we started him on blood-replacement fluids. I asked Margaret to go and wait upstairs so we could get on with the job and she left. Emma was invaluable. I had reached the point where, I'm afraid to say, my clinical judgement was becoming clouded by the attachment. She gently pointed out that perhaps it would be wise to X-ray his chest to make sure there was no spread before embarking on such radical surgery. She was right of course.

True to that week he, too, was full of that cruel spread of uncontrollable cells we call cancer. I slumped down in the theatre and just sobbed. How could I tell her? How could I ruin another person's life? I gathered myself as much as I could and walked upstairs to the house. I remember standing in the doorway to the living room and Margaret's cheerful, hopeful face turned towards me. All I could do was shake my head and nothing this time could stop the tears. She stood up and, as happens so often, became the one consoling me. The one who was prepared for the worst and was ready to start to deal with it.

We went down to the theatre and sat on a little ledge just in front of Elgar's face. His fluids had given him a little strength and he looked at us as we sat and cried and stroked his head and Margaret said goodbye. I will never forget the resigned, weary look on his face as he looked at his mistress. And I will *never* forget the way he seemed to muster all his strength, lift his head to look her level in the eye and wagged his tail. He was saying goodbye too.

The Bright Side

You see, on the whole, programmes like ours and *Animal Hospital* and *Pet Rescue* and *All Creatures Great and Small* are unable to show you the reality of the job. I know Rolf and I have occasionally shed a tear on television but there is *nothing* in this world that could have prepared me for the sheer anguish of that week. Just imagine how all those owners must have felt.

The fact is, though, that no matter how distressing that was for me I made a difference. I live in hope that I can make these people's suffering and that of their animals just that little bit easier. That is why I do my job. Regardless of the boredom and the heartsinkers and the hours and the bites and the scratches and the nights without sleep there are few jobs I can think of that in one way or another have the power to change people's and animals' lives the way you can as a vet.

The nights where you get home and you are tired and stressed and worrying and then you find a small, encrusted piece of unnameable crud stuck to your hand are nights filled with an astonishing sense of satisfaction. I know I have moaned about some of the people I have to deal with but, as I keep saying, they are a very small minority. As is so often true in life it is easy to remember the bad and forget the good. It is for people like Edwina, Felicity, Caroline, Martin and Margaret that I get up every day and go to work. They are the people that constantly restore my faith in human nature. They are the ones who you know will listen and learn and will do everything in their power to make sure their animal is OK. Inevitably I am naming just a handful but there are hundreds of others, characters that have enriched my life in so many ways, and as I think back over the last ten years there are more and more that come to mind. And, of course, the real stars of the show – their animals.

It is the small things as well as the life-saving surgery that make it a great job. The smiles of relief on an owner's face when you tell them everything is going to be OK; the lab test result that says everything is all clear; the new client who came because they were fed up with people telling them how good your service is; the way a dog drags his owner into the surgery because he can't wait to come and see you; the first lick in the face a new puppy gives you and the milky smell of its breath; the thank-you cards from the people you have helped and those that have touchingly been 'signed' on behalf of the pet; the ache in your arms and the tidemark of placental juices after a difficult calving; the first breath a kitten takes when you release it from its uterus during a caesarean and the first squeak it makes as it tries to call its mum; the sight of an animal tucking into its first meal after an operation; the look of trust on a dog's face as you inject an anaesthetic; the first steps a lamb takes towards the teat...

It is these small moments of magic that drop out of the air and into your life that make the job so worthwhile. And it is these moments that I live for. I became a vet because I wanted to help animals and it is the subtle expressions and nuances that they possess and the love that they bestow upon us even when we are not worthy that makes me love them more than ever.

So there you have it, the bare facts. I hope you're not disappointed but I also hope that you can now decide whether you are ready for the relentless onslaught of emotions that is inextricably entwined with being a vet.

How to Find the Right Vet

Over the years, I suppose because I have gained a reputation for speaking out on various issues, lots of people have tried to get me on board for their various campaigns. Everyone has a bandwagon that they would love to get a celebrity (no matter how far down the celebrity alphabet) on board. I have always given these issues consideration and have helped some but not others. One area that was tried is the veterinary profession itself. A lobby group wanted me on board to have a go at the profession. The reason I haven't is this: I have been qualified ten years, which, in the grand scheme of things, is a relatively short space of time. I do not consider myself qualified to judge other people in the profession. I also think it is very easy when freshly qualified to judge more senior members of the profession but this comes hand in hand with a naivety about the job itself.

The truth is that the vast majority of the profession are hard-working and very caring individuals trying to do an increasingly difficult job. However, as with all groups of people, there will always be that small minority who will leave a little to be desired, or indeed a lot in some cases! The difficulty faced by those trying to bring the bad apples to book is that of evidence and the way that the two sides to every story can be viewed from completely different perspectives. I have pondered this on numerous occasions and thought that surely they could go on the number of complaints that have been received about certain vets. However, after a programme I was involved in about British bulldogs, the Royal College of Veterinary Surgeons (RCVS) received a high number of complaints about me, but I certainly don't believe I should be struck off because of it.

The RCVS is always looking at ways to improve the overall performance of its 'offspring'. There is much more onus nowadays on vets to take on CPD (continuing professional development) and to keep up with current trends and practices. The RCVS has also now introduced the Practice Standards Scheme which will also help to foster improved standards and clinical excellence and help point owners to the best practices. Times are indeed changing and it will become harder for the bad apples to hide.

What I would say is if you are not happy with your vet for any reason voice your concerns. This doesn't have to be straight to the RCVS; it could be to the vet concerned or a senior member of staff at the same practice. If this avenue leaves you unsatisfied, then you can pursue it further with an official complaint. It may be that once you discuss the issue with your vet you realise there was a misunderstanding on one side or the other. Your vet may be merrily tripping along thinking you are completely happy with the service and the advice you have been given to that point.

The other option is always a second opinion. Over the years I have been asked to give a second opinion on an animal dozens of times and the owners invariably seem very guilty about what they are doing, as if they are in some way betraying their vet. All vets are flattered to have loyal clients, but most vets understand if you would like a second opinion and you are more than within your rights to seek one. If the vet you see concurs with your vet there is absolutely no reason why you shouldn't return to your original vet. It would be a very foolhardy vet who turns away business because of dented pride. It is also sometimes the case that a fresh pair of eyes, particularly in long-standing cases, can be useful. If you don't want to feel like a total defector make an excuse to see another vet in the same practice.

So how do you go about finding a good vet? I realised as I was going through this section that there are very few ways of knowing for sure before you have a problem whether you have a good vet or not. One of the most difficult things is moving to a new area and having to find a new vet, especially if you are leaving one you really trust.

Word of mouth is a very informative tool. If you are moving to a new area ask your old vet if he can recommend anyone. As I have intimated, the veterinary profession is a relatively small community. Many vets will know someone or a friend of a friend in many areas of the country. Your vet may well be able to give you a personal recommendation and will probably be pleased to steer you in the right direction. If this is not the case, then ask the people where you move to. This may sound like an obvious thing to say but many of us do not talk to neighbours when we move. Ask ten different people, ask as many as you can. If you have dogs you will usually find that dog-walking encounters are excellent sources of information. Within weeks of moving to the village where I live now, the local dog walkers had informed me of all the best places to walk. One woman even took me and showed me herself!

Another possibility when you move to a new area, is to ring up a few practices. Ask them any questions you may have like appointment times, out-of-hours services and so on, and then, at the end of the call, ask if there are any other vets they would recommend. I know this sounds stupid, but the truth is that a vet is not likely to recommend another vet in the area whom he or she knows to be as useful as a wet rag. None of them will be expecting this question but I don't see any reason why you shouldn't ask it. I'm sure you will soon build up a picture of the ones in the *Yellow Pages* that no one has mentioned to you.

Once you've found one or two that you are interested in, ask if you can come on a visit. By dropping in you will get an idea of the atmosphere of the place, you'll be able to chat to the staff and have a look round the whole premises. If they are cagey or reluctant for you to see behind closed doors then there may be good reason.

It is a minefield to some degree and experience is the most telling thing. That is why the opinion of other pet owners is so important. You can draw on their experience. But remember, though, most of us are genuinely trying our best to help you and your pets.

PART THREE
THE TRUTH ABOUT DOGS

Pan and Badger

Pan.

© Emma Milne

Badger.

© Emma Milne

I've come to the part where I want to talk about my main motivation for writing the book and I must warn you in advance that I may get quite heated. What I am about to tell you is so blindingly obvious it is ridiculous. It is the simplest common sense. The fact is that we have become accustomed over time to the way our dogs and, now to a lesser degree, our cats look. What I hope you will see by the end of this book is that this has gone way too far and we have effectively taken highly successful species and turned them into an array of mutated and often unhealthy caricatures of what they once were. Indeed, a paper by McGreevy and Nicholas in 1999 states that 'Some breed standards and selection practices run counter to the welfare interests of dogs, to the extent that some breeds are characterised by traits that may be difficult to defend on welfare grounds.'

I said at the beginning of the book that much of what is here is based on anecdotes from my time in practice or trawled from my clients and friends. I deliberately set out *not* to make this book a highly scientific reference work because I want it to be accessible to all. There are absolutely countless articles on the conditions and problems I want to highlight. I will reference some because I want you to see that it is far from true that no one knows about these things. The trouble is that many of these works are produced with vets in mind and can be highly unreadable to anyone without a good knowledge of medical and veterinary jargon or a good working knowledge of Latin!

Where better to start than with my own dogs, Pan and Badger. I've been wanting to tell you about Pan and Badger for some time now and haven't really found a convenient place to do it. This seems as good a time as any. I am about to extol the virtues of mongrels and seeing as 'the boys' are two of the most wonderful mongrels I have had the good fortune to come across in my entire life they should fit right in here. People are always asking me what they are. They are a fairly distinctive couple and have been recognised in their own right probably more times that I have. They are the reason that I get out of bed on horrible winter mornings and walk three miles in the pouring rain. They are quite simply the centre of my life and I am boringly obsessed with them.

I have had them for ten years now and I have, over this time, worked out what all the components of them are. We'll start with Badger. He has the coat of a Border collie, that much is certain. His ears resemble a set of handlebars and are always at half mast. He has the 'point' of a pointer. He has the eyes of a hawk and can spot a rabbit at several hundred yards. This rabbit, along with all its friends, is very safe because Badger is a New Age man. He loves small furry creatures and all he wants to do is lick their bottoms and simply sit and watch them for as long as is humanly (or doggedly) possible. He has the elegance and speed of a cheetah and when he changes from fourth gear into fifth he fluidly flattens his body into one beautiful, streamlined vision and turns into a black-and-white blur. He always has a slightly gormless expression because his mouth is always slightly open with a quizzical look in his eye. He lives and loves to run.

Pan is quite a different creature. He has the eyes of a wolf and when he fixes you with those beautiful, orange eyes he seems to look right inside you. He has the coat of a husky crossed with a bear. He has the high rump and sprinting speed of a thoroughbred racehorse combined with about as much stamina as a man trying to make love after ten pints. Rabbits are safe from him too. Not through any caring desire that he has to study them but simply because he runs about like a headless chicken and doesn't even see most of them. He has the tail of Basil Brush. He has the appetite of a Labrador. He lives and loves to eat and no unguarded bin is safe from him.

Pan and Badger.
© Emma Milne

Separately they are beautiful, stunning dogs but together they are a priceless unit. They are completely inseparable. They refuse steadfastly to play with other dogs and if another dog is running with them they simply ignore it. If it gets in the way of their game they scornfully grumble at it and then resume whatever they were doing. Their favourite pastime is the twig game. Pan will very pointedly find a small twig and hold it very delicately in his teeth and will wait until Badger notices he's got it. If Badger is pretending he hasn't seen him, Pan will run on the spot staring at him and start whining. Badger will then start to run away from him and

69

commence his attack from a wide arc. He will canter until he is within striking distance and directly behind Pan, and then he will change gear and flatten out to full speed. Pan will wait for him and watch him out of the corner of his eye and then duck to one side right at the last minute. Badger will fly past him, teeth snapping wildly in mid-air as he pretends he was really trying to get the stick. This will continue for several attack-cum-runs. At some point Pan will get bored and lay down and just start chewing the twig. Badger will commence his run but when he realises Pan is not going to run away he will simply start 'springing'. This is another of Badger's particular talents, during which he resembles a slightly gormless antelope with handlebar ears. He springs round Pan in big, four-feet-off-the-floor jumps and wildly snaps his teeth in the air. Pan steadfastly ignores him until the twig is shredded and will then casually get up and saunter off. Badger will stare after him with a disappointed look for several seconds and eventually give up and follow him.

They trot along with a loping gait and are often touching flanks as they go. At some telepathic point, only started by some unique, unseen signal between them, they will run at full speed to a completely empty tree where they once saw a squirrel five months previously and leap repeatedly up at the tree barking wildly. This usually ends when Pan decides for no particular reason to savage Badger playfully in the side of the neck. At this point they will both stop and just stare into the distance for a few seconds and then trot off together. Pan likes to savage Badger in the neck quite frequently for no apparent reason even when there are no invisible squirrels involved. Badger's revenge for this is his particular pièce de résistance. We call it his 'zebra-take-down-manoeuvre'.

It all starts with the dogs leaping about and wrestling like boxing hares. There will be a lot of scruff pulling and leg-chewing on both parts. At any opportune moment when Pan's rump presents itself Badger will go for the kill. He seizes a painfully large-looking piece of Pan's flesh on his back. The exact location of this piece of flesh is critical for the manoeuvre to work. It has to be just far enough back for Pan to be unable to turn and reach him and right on top to make it even more difficult. Pan twists and turns and tries to shake him off but Badger has a lot of savaging to make up for and hangs on in a spirited fashion. Eventually Pan succumbs as a zebra does to a lion and crashes to the floor in an agonising

70

feigned death roll. Badger, victorious, will immediately straddle the prone and upturned Pan and set about him. His point proved, they will then decide to go and look for some small, furry things of one sort or another and trot off amicably, sides touching, tongues lolling and with a very contented air about them.

No matter what mood I am in, they always make me smile. They never sulk because I am moody. They are always there to put a head on my knee when I am upset and they can always be relied upon to jump directly and accurately onto your bladder when they are allowed upstairs for a cuddle on special occasions.

So what are they? They are dogs.

Badger and Pan redolent in the evening sun.
© Emma Milne

71

Designer Pets and the Breed Standard

As I mentioned earlier I went into the veterinary course and the job in a blinkered and naive way and I should have taken more note of the subtle digs that were made at university by our very eminent teaching staff. There were countless occasions when lecturers made concerned comments about particular breeds and, more commonly, slight digs about the people that continue to produce them. It's strange that it never really struck me at the time how preposterous it was that we, as a profession, didn't have more to say about this. It wasn't until I qualified and started to see these poor animals on a daily basis that I started to realise just how appalling it all is.

I have often asked myself, and occasionally been asked by others who have been amazed by these revelations, why vets don't say more about it. Vets actually do talk about it a lot. We have whole books and journals and lecture courses devoted to it. We know that our most powerful diagnostic tool is breed type and many vets when discussing particular breed problems are as mortified as I am. I'm sure many responsible breeders feel the same. The trouble with us vets is that we are stuck between a rock and a hard place. The vast majority of the time we do not see the animals concerned until *after* the point of sale. People looking to buy a certain breed naturally go to pet-shop book sections or talk to breeders or breed enthusiasts rather than talk to their vet. These former outlets may not be very forthcoming when it comes to the matter of breed health problems. Some people may not even have a vet until they have purchased their pet. I think many people still view us as somewhere you go when you have a problem, not as a source of advice before owning a pet. In fact, on the Kennel Club's own website when advising potential breeders about how to find out about health issues with particular breeds it states:

'Before breeding from a dog or bitch, the Kennel Club advises breeders to investigate whether there are any possible inherited conditions that may affect the breed. Breeders can do this by discussing the matter with the breeder of their dog, the relevant breed club or clubs, the Kennel Club Health & Information Department or, possibly, their veterinary surgeon.'

Statements like this do little to promote vets as a source of information, not just for breeders but for prospective owners. We are, after all, on the front line, so to speak, and are the ones seeing and dealing with the health 'fall out' from these breeds on a daily basis. Talking to your vet *prior* to purchase could save you untold heartache as well as money.

There is little point in us as vets becoming exasperated at an owner who lovingly brings in their new charge because they were none the wiser. In later life, if a disease or condition starts, there is little to be gained from pointing out that you knew they would have these problems because it is obviously too late. Many vets feel they are in a very difficult position when it comes to breed-related problems and issues such as tail docking. It would be wrong to alienate clients by being angry with them because it is usually not their fault. It is also detrimental to the welfare of the dog or cat because if a client feels they are going to get badgered and chastised every time they go to the vet they simply won't go. It angers me when people say vets keep quiet about it because they make so much money from these problems. I'm pretty sure most vets would rather be involved with healthy dogs requiring emergency care or preventative medicine than spending most of the time addressing vanity-induced problems.

Emily, whom I mentioned before, lives in France. A few years ago she sent me a book, knowing what my feelings were on these subjects. It is in French and is called *Un Vétérinaire en Colère: Essai sur la condition animale* by Charles Danten. The title translates as *An Angry Vet: Essay on the animal condition*. The front cover features a picture of a basset hound with a ball and chain round one of its legs. My French extends to GCSE level and get-by-holiday French but I started to translate the book. It is written by a vet and echoes many of my feelings and sentiments. It was a relief to me to see that I was not the only one and since then I have talked to numerous people, vets, breeders and public who all feel the same. It is time to do something about it.

You only have to look at the advertising for veterinary products that is aimed at vets to see how widespread the evidence of these diseases is among certain breeds. For example, there is a very good shampoo that is for bacterial, fungal and yeast infections of the skin. The dogs used in the advert are the basset hound and the westie. An antibacterial, anti-inflammatory skin cream will be sold with a picture of a Shar Pei or a bulldog. Painkillers for long-term arthritis will be advertised with a retriever. A drug for congestive heart failure will be advertised with a picture of a Cavalier King Charles spaniel.

As I said earlier, much of the information in this book is based on my own experience and there will be some that say that it is unreferenced and unscientific and, therefore, hearsay. I was thinking about specific texts I could put in a list of references to support what I say (*see pages* 179–84). One of the books I have referenced is Gough and Thomas's *Breed Predispositions to Disease in Dogs and Cats*. Right at the beginning of their introduction the authors state: 'It is well known that most breeds of dogs and cats have diseases to which they are prone. Breed predispositions are often listed under specific disease conditions in the published literature and textbooks. However, it is hard to find a source of information that lists these conditions by breed.' This is an important point and one that I myself encountered when considering which texts to include in the references. The fact is that *every* single veterinary clinical textbook will have breed predispositions in them. They are so widely accepted and known about that there are virtually no books devoted solely to the subject because these diseases and conditions are so inextricably linked with our pedigrees.

To illustrate my point I just went into our office where we keep our journals and text books and grabbed a totally random handful. The front cover of the June 2005 edition of the *Journal of Small Animal Practice* advertises the following article titles: 'Gastrointestinal problems associated with upper respiratory tract disease in *brachycephalic breeds*', 'Review of neurological diseases in the *Cavalier King Charles spaniel*', 'Suspected hereditary sensory neuropathy in two *Border collie* puppies' and 'Cerebellar cortical degeneration in *English bulldogs*' (my italics throughout). The *European Journal of Companion Animal Practice* from April 2005 has a report on the whole FECAVA *Hereditary Disease* Symposium

(FECAVA stands for Federation of European Companion Animal Veterinary Associations). The *In Practice* journal from October 2000 has an article entitled 'Canine dilated cardiomyopathy: *breed manifestations* and diagnosis'. I could go on, but you get the point. If I wanted to give you a recommended reading list I'd have to give you the entire veterinary library worldwide.

Unfortunately as time has gone by I started to realise that much of what I was doing was spending a vast majority of my time sorting out the problems that the likes of the Kennel Club have created. And let's be frank, most of these problems have been created, even if accidentally, so that we as a species can have our designer dogs and cats.

I have to say that the Kennel Club (not just the British one but all kennel clubs and the cat equivalents) is going to come in for a bashing here because they are the governing body of pedigreed dogs in this country. They are the ones that have selected these dogs to the nth degree. Some breeders are also going to be very unhappy about my 'sweeping generalisations' and some owners are going to be upset because they love a certain breed and will have no bad word said against them. So let's get things straight.

The Kennel Club, in conjunction with organisations such as the British Veterinary Association (BVA) has a number of health schemes in place to try to reduce inherited problems. This is a good thing without question, but do they go far enough? The truth is that, to my mind, some of these breeds can never be considered healthy until their conformation is dramatically changed. By 'conformation' I mean the size and shape of various body regions in relation to each other and the animal's general appearance. Conformation is dictated by the breed standards.

These health schemes have been put in place and, in the UK, left entirely to the breeders' discretion as to whether they actually participate or not. A perfect example is the hip dysplasia scheme. We have a large number of breeds such as the Labrador and the German shepherd dog that suffer from this potentially crippling condition. The hip dysplasia scheme was first introduced in 1978 for the German shepherd dog to try to ensure that only dogs with good hips were bred from. Many other breeds were added to the scheme and there are now data for 118 breeds. In the time the scheme has been running awareness has been raised to some degree and the occurrence of the condition in the two breeds I mentioned previously has dropped a little in the UK. However, screening is not compulsory. Surely, if the Kennel Club, at the start of the scheme, had said that no puppies from the breeds on the scheme could be registered unless the parents had both been certified and had *good* hips the rate of change would have been much quicker.

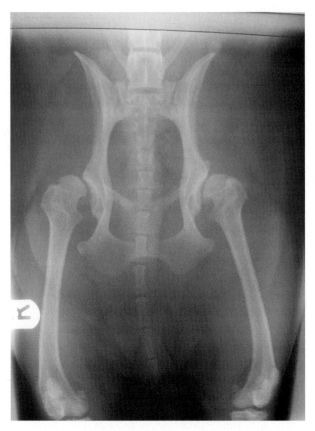

German shepherd dog with severe dysplasia.
© Mark Goodman

I had a client when I worked in Cheltenham who came in with a Labrador at the age of twelve months because she was a little lame on her back legs. After some examinations we decided it would be best to X-ray her hips. This was partly because hip dysplasia was high on the list of possibilities but also because the owner wanted to breed from her and we strongly advised hip scoring before he made the choice. This way we could do both things at the same time. The screening involves an X-ray of the hips and pelvis and this is sent away to the BVA where certain measurements are taken. A score is recorded out of a possible 106, the lower the score the better, and the advice is that no dog should be bred from that has a score that is not *well below* the breed mean score.

In the event, we didn't really need to send her X-rays off to see the problem. Her hip conformation was awful. She already had signs of arthritis around her joints and we knew she was facing a lifetime of medication and possibly major surgery. We sent the X-rays to the BVA because gathering this data is very important. The highest recorded score for the breed is 106; this dog's was 96. Her owners were mortified and quite understandably so. He told me that they had never had a dog before and had tried to do everything right by getting a pedigree. He had even paid extra for a longer pedigree history! How bloody ironic! He simply couldn't understand how, if such a scheme was in place, the puppies could have been registered without the necessary tests being done on the parents. I had no answer for him; I couldn't understand it either.

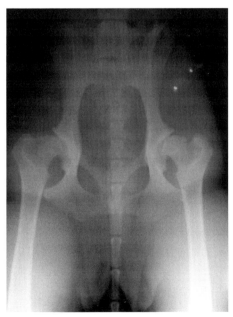

Labrador with a hip score of 96.
© Emma Milne

There are a couple of important points to make here regarding the schemes. The hip dysplasia scheme is a very good database of information for breeders and vets but there is every chance that it is skewed to reflect average scores that are actually better than those of the whole population. You see, it is reasonable to suggest that many people with dogs that have visibly poor hips on X-ray will not bother to have them scored. Therefore only the better ones will get entered onto the database. The other point worth noting is that the scheme does not seem to have made a massive difference to the scores relative to how long it has been in place. Indeed the well-known geneticist, Dr Malcolm Willis states that:

> Progress is minimal but that is not a reflection of the merits of the scheme but simply illustrates that selection is not being practised to any degree. In countries where schemes involve compulsion i.e. that one cannot breed from (and register) specific levels of hip status (as in Scandinavia) or where there is peer and club pressure such that untested dogs cannot be shown ... there is evidence of progress. However, in the UK and USA where breeders are free to do as they please progress is not usually seen and there is minimal advance.

Some time ago I was interviewed by a man from a pro-pedigree magazine. We have locked horns before and I wasn't relishing the conversation. The last time we spoke a couple of years ago he suggested to me that one reason I probably saw more pedigrees at the surgery was because the owners of pedigree dogs care more about them and are therefore more likely to seek veterinary attention. I think this is possibly one of the most offensive notions I have ever had put to me and I'm sure many of you moggy and mongrel owners out there will feel the same. He also lambasted me for being interviewed on a television programme about pedigrees and failing to mention the health schemes run by the Kennel Club. I pointed out that, as an interviewee on a ten-minute piece, I had little control over what parts of three hours of interview were included and that I had actually gone into the schemes in some depth but that particular section was cut. Whether he believed me or not I don't really care but I told him that was precisely why I was writing this book.

I went on to relate to him the story about the Labrador cited above. His reaction to this was that the man who bought the dog was at fault because he should have properly researched it before buying the dog. This is my *entire* point. All the time there is the continued misconception that the word 'pedigree' plus the exchange of a large sum of cash equals a healthy dog, why on earth would anyone question it? How can we expect the public to go into all these things when no one will admit the breeds have any problems? There are countless books about all the various breeds where this poor guy could have gone to do his research. Would any of them written by lovers of the breeds that have 'no problems' include such information?

Over the years the Kennel Club has often refuted what I have said about pedigrees having around 400 inherited and congenital diseases. This seems a little strange when in April 2005 their own geneticist Dr Jeff Sampson wrote in the *European Journal of Companion Animal Practice* that:

> Unfortunately, the restrictive breeding patterns that have developed as part and parcel of the purebred dog scene have not been without collateral damage to all breeds. This is particularly true in the area of inherited disease. In excess of 350 inherited diseases have been described in the purebred dog population, and many of these are restricted to particular breeds or groups of related breeds.

He goes on to say: 'Increasingly, inherited diseases are imposing a serious disease burden on most, if not all, breeds of dog.' Let there be no doubt that these problems are extremely well documented by veterinary surgeons and geneticists the world over.

Let's just say that the Kennel Club attitude to improving the health of these animals falls way short of what I, as a vet, expect from the governing body of all our pedigrees. Yes, a proportion of the blame must fall at the feet of some of the breeders. I must say here that I do know that many, many breeders are caring and honest and are genuinely and unreservedly in it for the love of the breed. Just this week I was reading a cat magazine at the surgery and there was a letter from a Persian breeder of twenty-plus years. She was quite rightly upset at the new trend of the most preposterously flat faces the breed has ever seen. She was imploring people to have some sort of perspective on this and to reverse this alarming trend.

One of my former clients in Somerset is a breeder of British shorthairs. She was totally devastated one day to find a three-year-old cat of hers dead in her run. The cat had died of heart failure but had shown no signs of illness. The lady immediately stopped breeding until she had had every one of her cats scanned for heart disease. She also got in touch with people she knew had offspring and warned them. The point is I *know* there are good and bad in all things. However, everyone will tell me and you that all the problems are down to the irresponsible and disreputable breeders. What would be the best way of putting off the money-grabbing, uncaring or simply ignorant minority? MAKE IT COMPULSORY FOR THEM TO INVEST IN THE AVAILABLE HEALTH SCHEMES!

At the time of writing there are also currently approximately twenty DNA tests available worldwide for roughly forty breeds of dog and cat. I use the words 'approximately' and 'roughly' because the numbers of tests being developed and indeed the number of diseases being discovered are changing all the time. These tests are designed to identify carriers of known inherited disease and thus allow people to make educated decisions about whether to breed from certain individuals.

Despite all of this I want to show you that some of these breeds by their very shape and conformation are unnatural and therefore inherently unhealthy. No matter how careful you are, unless the breeds are changed morphologically they can never be viewed as truly healthy or 'normal'.

I have come under a lot of criticism for my pedigree bashing. Don't misunderstand me, I love all animals. I still loved Chaucer the pug I told you about earlier. It's not his fault he lost an eye and his skin folds were constantly infected and he couldn't breathe properly. You saw in the introduction that when I qualified I, along with the rest of my year, took an oath similar to the one doctors do. I pledged to safeguard the welfare of all animals in my care. I stick by this unconditionally. I don't see dogs as one breed or another. I am not a dog or cat racist. During the time that I was involved with the new Animal Welfare Bill and particularly tail docking I received an email via the Vets Against Docking website from an irate man who said, among his ranting about how stupid poodles look with tails (don't get me started, we'll be addressing that later), that, 'As a vet, you should want to keep breed standards up. If you don't agree with keeping breed standards up, then do you think it's OK to mix breeds?' It may be far fetched but it all smacks a bit of an animal KKK attitude to me. I wonder what Hitler's breed standard for the master race would have been? Don't get me wrong, I wouldn't for a second mean to compare the horrors of the Nazis or the KKK to dog breeding but when I get emails like that it does make we wonder how sane some people are.

What I am very tired of is spending my time alleviating the misery created by what basically boils down to people's wishes to have an accessory or status symbol and win prizes for it. We couldn't even draw cartoons of most of our dog breeds any more because they have come to resemble the cartoons. Of course I don't want to see the end of our pedigrees, I just want them to be healthy and I want the extremes to be addressed.

All of this is in the name of the 'breed standard'. This is what is set down by the Kennel Club and tells you what you should look for in any individual of any breed. As we progress I hope you will start to share my incredulity at how we can possibly say what a dog 'should' look like. They're dogs, aren't they? Well, they used to be before utility and purpose went out the window and the 'breed standard' became the most important thing. Dr Jeff Sampson, in the same article quoted earlier says, that, '... it is likely that for most of dogs' time on earth, there were just general types of dogs, hunting, guarding and herding. The concept of distinct breeds is a very recent development in man's association with the dog, with most of our modern breeds of dogs having existed for fewer than 400 years.'

At this point I would like to point out that I want to be accurate so I did something that took a lot of will-power. I parted with £24.50 of my hard-earned cash and put it in the pocket of the Kennel Club. That's right, I bought the *Illustrated Breed Standards* book. If any of you want to verify my quotes I suggest you borrow the book from the library to avoid funding the process. I will consult the 'good book' as we proceed to illustrate my points.

So where shall we begin our journey into the world of the pedigree animal?

I think we should start with a little genetics and a look at how our dogs came about.

Survival of the Fittest

Most of you will be aware of the discoveries made by a man called Charles Darwin. He basically came up with the theory of evolution and the principle of the survival of the fittest. He was a pretty bright guy. I wonder if he turns in his grave when he sees what we have done with his theory.

The logic of the theory is that in any group of animals the fittest ones will survive. This may mean the most intelligent or it may mean the one with the best camouflage or the biggest horns or the most brute strength. Regardless, it is these animals that will eventually procreate and pass their genes on to the next generation. In this way evolution occurs. The animals with the traits that make them survive the best get their genetic material continued. It makes perfect sense and sounds very obvious now we are all so accustomed to the theory. What I aim to show you is that none of our breeds would exist in a natural environment. They would simply become one big hotch-potch of beautiful, healthy mongrels.

I don't want to get too technical here but we need a basic understanding of why before we can continue. We are all aware of the fact that it is not considered proper in our society to marry our relatives or have children with them. This may be undesirable because your brother looks like the arse end of a rhino, but there is a very simple, genetic reason for this and that is the problems that can be associated with inbreeding.

Every group of animals is made up of a gene pool. This is the genetic material contained in that group. To remain healthy animals rely on a large gene pool to ensure that undesirable traits and deficiencies aren't continued or are so rarely expressed as to be negligible. Related animals share some of the same genes. If these animals mate with each other time and again throughout generations the gene pool becomes more and more concentrated. It's kind of like a stagnant pond. If no running water is added it eventually evaporates into a small sludge of useless gunge. Cross-breeds tend to end up with the best traits from the parents and the ones that don't by chance will often not survive.

Genetics can be very basically subdivided into dominant and recessive genes. When two animals mate the offspring will get one gene for a certain trait, such as coat colour, from the mother and one from the father. A dominant gene is one that will produce its trait in the offspring. For example, brown eye colour in humans is dominant to blue so the only way you can get blue eyes is if a child gets one recessive gene from each parent because if either is the gene for brown the eyes will be brown. Other examples of dominant genes are those for short hair in cats, black coat colour in dogs and, more recently, polycystic kidney disease in some cats, particularly Persians.

In the case of the last example where the dominant gene is for a disease or defect these genes will tend to be self-limiting because they will always produce the defect or disease and will cause death. This is the reason that defects caused by dominant genes are readily identified and can be dealt with because their effects and presence are so obvious. However, the problem with our pure breeds is those pesky and often hidden recessive genes. These are trouble because unless both inherited genes are the recessive form the trait or defect will not be shown and can be unwittingly passed on to future generations. In the wild this does not tend to cause too many problems because the chances of the recessive genes ending up together are so slim in a large gene pool. The problem with pedigrees that are inbred is that over time these pools have become smaller and smaller and recessive genes for defects have started to make their presence known.

The other big issue these days is that the visible characteristics that we have selected for that are deemed to be desirable in the show ring have unwittingly selected for disease at the same time. The other problem with this is the genetic bottleneck that is created by show champion dogs. These dogs become highly sought after as stud dogs and end up fathering a very large number of offspring. This then tends to mean that as generations go by there becomes an increasing likelihood of related animals being mated time and again. A prime example of this is the standard poodle. Back in the 1950s and 60s in the States the Wycliffe Kennel engaged in huge inbreeding and line breeding between its closely related champion standard poodles. The Wycliffe line has reached far and wide and produced a huge genetic bottleneck. In fact, the practice of line breeding where very closely related animals are mated together is fairly commonplace even today.

If you have a family of animals that carry the gene for a particular disease and you mate them with a member of an unaffected family, for simplicity's sake, let's say that the chance of the young developing the disease is halved. However, mate them with another member of the same family and the chance is doubled. It is these fundamental laws that we have looked at, dismissed and thrown out of the nearest window when it comes to man's best friend. Ironic, really, that we have wantonly played havoc with the one species we claim to love the most.

In practice I found myself becoming increasingly frustrated with the owners of these dogs. In a very short space of time I realised that it is not their fault. The vast majority of people in this country are still being lied to by the 'manufacturers' of these animals. There is still a massive misapprehension that the word 'pedigree' denotes a highly bred and healthy animal. After all, we pay enough for them, don't we? Countless people come to me for their pet's first vaccination and proudly present me with its fourteen generation pedigree certificate with a big proud grin on their face. It is usually at this moment that I try as hard as I can not to run screaming from the room, knowing that in six months' time they will be back with some problem or other that is going to persist for the rest of the poor bloody thing's life. Sadly, in some cases, not a very long life.

Any vet will tell you that a mongrel, in general, will be healthier than a pedigree. Some of you might argue back and say things like, 'Well, if you cross a German shepherd and a Labrador you could still get hip problems, couldn't you?' Of course you could. Just listen. I'm talking about proper mutts. Heinz 57s. Dogs that you look at and can't really tell any more what they started out as. All you need to know is that it is a dog.

And don't write to me telling me that you had a mongrel and it spent the whole of its life at the vets. Of course there are no guarantees. I am speaking in general terms.

'Devolution' of the Modern Dog

I have called this 'devolution' because no such distinct breeds would exist without human intervention and selection. There are hundreds of recognised breeds of dog these days and they are so distinct physically that they can be clearly identified as a certain breed just by looking at them. This unnatural selection is responsible for the high levels of disease we see today in these breeds.

Most people know that our domestic dogs are descended from wolves. Wolves are one of the most successful species in the history of the planet. They are intelligent and fit and very adaptable. It is these traits that made them perfect candidates to spawn the domestic dog. This is where it gets very obvious. Compare a wolf to the utterly dreadful Pekinese that won Crufts in recent years. The poor thing could barely breathe, walk, blink or groom itself! Chances of survival unaided: none.

Somehow the Kennel Club in its infinite wisdom deemed this to be the best dog in the world. That is what the winner of Crufts is supposed to be, isn't it? Peter Purves and the American who commentate on the programme couldn't stop going on about the fact that the handler didn't let him cut any corners. Oh no, he was such a brave and strong little dog that he could make it all the way round a ring. WHAT!!!! Should we not expect a healthy dog to be able to trot forty yards without collapsing and gasping for air?

I must admit that I did have a chuckle to myself when the man taking him round the ring had just finished grooming him for the six-hundredth time that day ready for one last drag round the ring and the dog took a brief second and shook vigorously and completely ruined its perfectly coiffed mane. It gave me the same pleasure I get when I hear that a matador has been gored by the bull he's been tormenting for the last hour.

The fact is that dogs were not originally domesticated because ancient man thought they were *cute*. They were domesticated for a purpose. We needed them to help us hunt and guard our camps and pull our sleds. This is where all our breeds originated. They all had a purpose and this is where the subtle changes in their appearance began.

For example, a small dog is needed to hunt rabbits so that it can fit down a hole. A large, strong dog is needed to hunt deer and a dog with a very thick coat is needed if it is to survive in Alaska. This may sound like a trite thing to say but it is what happened over the next few hundred years that takes the biscuit. It's quite clever really how they got away with it for so long. Do it gradually so no one notices and at some point it will just be accepted. Well, I am not going to accept it any more.

The trouble is that as time went by and we evolved to the point where we didn't really *need* dogs for most of the things they were bred for, the powers that be had to find some other use for them. As it turned out it was just to see who had the 'best' one. It is pretty difficult to pick one identical dog from another so I imagine this is where the concept of the breed standard came from. If you decide what a perfect example of a breed should be then you can give people something to aim for. There is a paragraph at the beginning of 'the book' that goes like this: 'These standards are an essential guide for all breeders, exhibitors and judges of pedigree dogs. They endeavour to provide the description of the perfect example of each breed.' As you will see as we progress, some of the criteria actually deemed desirable in a 'perfect' example of some of these breeds are, without doubt, unhealthy defects that we, as vets, would note during a clinical examination of a 'normal' crossbreed.

This point is very obvious when you compare show strains of some breeds with working strains. I recently had a field cocker spaniel in for a booster and its shape was very different to what most people see as a cocker spaniel. The ears were smaller, legs longer and overall shape much more proportioned. Labrador enthusiasts will also readily point out the differences between showers and workers.

Back to the story. What happened next is that the standards became more and more exaggerated over time and this is what has destroyed our dogs. The characteristics that made them useful in the first place have been their downfall. The fact that a dachshund had a slightly long back and short legs to get down holes has now been stretched to the point that most of them barely have a gap between their stomachs and the floor and so are extremely prone to spinal problems.

Many of the inbred problems with our pedigrees are ones of bad conformation. As we have altered the size and shape of certain features we have altered the most fundamental thing about successful animals and that is proportion. We have accentuated features and distorted the form that nature intended. There are hundreds of examples of this but I will tell you about some of the worst ones as examples. You can then apply the logic to almost any dog.

Long Bodies and Shortened Limbs

Many of our breeds of dog have bodies that are relatively long compared not only to the strength and size of the rest of the dog but also to the length of the limbs. The problem with this is partly a matter of mechanics and engineering and partly one of genetic manipulation of growth. If you designed a bridge that had weak supports and a very long span it would fail without question. It is a fact that a long span must have support, either from the centre or from suspension. In these dogs there is no support for the span, which is the spine. The spine therefore is under an enormous amount of stress and ultimately becomes bowed and sagging. Many breeds have been 'engineered' this way such as the Basset family, Dandie Dinmont, Cesky terrier, Skye terrier, corgi and, most notably, the dachshund. According to the Kennel Club book 'the length of the back and the character of the discs between the vertebrae of the spine have a tendency to allow a weakening in the area, and it is therefore important that the loin should be short and strong, and that individuals should not be allowed to become obese.'

What it does not tell you is that dogs such as dachshunds and corgis are what we call 'chondrodystrophic' or 'achondroplastic'. These terms are a grand way of saying that the breeds cannot make cartilage properly. The trait is an inherited one. The 'weakening' that the Kennel Club book describes is where changed and abnormal cartilage making up the discs in the spine fail over time. This can cause progressive or sudden paralysis. The cartilage fails all over the body to a degree but it is most apparent in several areas of the back because of the stresses on the discs as the back flexes during normal movement. Many of these dogs require spinal surgery to have any hope of walking again and some have to be put to sleep because of the condition.

The fact that this trait is inherited should come as no surprise because we have actually selected for it over time. As Gough and

88

Jim the dachshund after spinal surgery.
© Julian Bainbridge

Thomas point out in their description of achondroplasia, 'achondroplastic breeds are specifically bred for this condition. They have short maxillae, flared metaphyses and short, bowed limbs. This is *accepted as part of the breed standard*' (my italics). To me, as with many of these conformational abnormalities that are now viewed as the norm, surely it should be unacceptable to deliberately breed a defect into an animal to provide a certain look. Intervertebral disc disease is the most common spinal disease we see in dogs and although not exclusive to chondrodystrophic breeds the defect is responsible for the partial and complete paralysis of many of these dogs a year.

As the definition stated above, chondrodystrophic breeds have short, bowed limbs. The selection for shortened limbs probably started for a reason when dogs were used for hunting rabbits, badgers, rats and the like, and needed to be able to get down holes of various sizes. What has happened now, with the passage of time and the continued selection for extremes of these traits, is that the bones in the legs have become twisted and deformed. If you look at X-rays of the legs of breeds such as the dachshund and the basset the bones are almost unrecognisable when compared to those of their distant ancestors. As the bones have become distorted the mechanical stresses and strains on the joints have changed. A 'normal', largely straight bone has evolved over the centuries with muscle attachments in exactly the right places to achieve very efficient movement and maximum strength. Joints fit well together and healthy cartilage ensures smooth and even movement of the joints.

In breeds with deformed legs and joints the muscles pull in an

89

abnormal way and the joint surfaces can no longer meet as they are intended to do. This, in turn, can cause the early onset of arthritis or degenerative joint disease because the joints do not function properly, the protective cartilage becomes eroded and the shock-absorbing joint fluid becomes thin and watery.

Besides the medical problems that these legs have created I can't help but be sad when I see dogs like this out walking. A while ago I was walking 'the boys' at a place called Crickley Hill near Cheltenham. We love it there and it is extremely beautiful. I was walking through a wooded section and thoroughly enjoying myself when a couple came towards me. At first I couldn't see any dogs, but about twenty yards past them I met their dogs – three Dandie Dinmonts. The three of them waddled past me at a very slow speed and they were barely clearing the ground as they laboured through the fallen leaves on their tiny pins. Badger and Pan trotted elegantly past them and totally ignored them because they were far too interested in where the next squirrel might appear. I stood and looked at the stark contrast between the way they moved and it just made me sad. I absolutely love to watch my dogs run. I love to see their obvious, unadulterated pleasure that comes from simply running. Sometimes Badger just tears about because he doesn't know what else to do. It makes my day every time. I know it's probably anthropomorphising these creatures but I can't help but wonder whether dogs that have problems running get frustrated seeing my two lope easily past them. It just makes me sad.

I love the Natural History Museum in London. I went on many school trips when I was a child and I have been back quite a few times since, usually dragging an unfortunate sister with me on the pretext of showing her something. Last time I was there I saw a display about evolution. It featured the usual show of ape to man and such like. However, it also showed a dachshund when the breed first appeared and one now. They are very different. There was no comment attached to it; it was an example of how breeding can select certain features. It made me realise that I was right that these dogs are still inexorably changing but also that no one seems to have actually noticed that we should be worried.

The Kennel Club book tells us that bassets originated in France where the term 'basset' refers to their short-leggedness. With a laughable sense of national pride, it also tells us that, although the basset originated in France, 'the breed was developed to perfection in Britain.' Well, let's all stand up and slap each other on the back. We have managed to 'perfectly' develop one of the most unhealthy, ungainly and potentially unhappy breeds there is. The book also tells us that, at only 38 centimetres high at the shoulder but weighing some 32 kilos, the dog is apparently 'quite difficult to pick up to put in a hatchback'. Perhaps we should be pondering whether legs this short and twisted are capable of comfortably carrying 32 kilos of weight and whether we should possibly expect a 'normal dog' to be able to get into a car unaided.

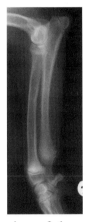

Side view of the radius
and ulna of a 'normal' dog.
© Andrew Moores

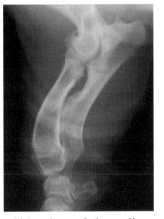

Side view of the radius
and ulna of a basset.
© Andrew Moores

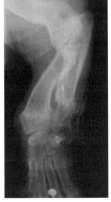

Front view of the radius
and ulna of a basset.
© Andrew Moores

Front view of the radius
and ulna of a 'normal' dog.
© Andrew Moores

Shortened legs, whether chondrodystrophoid or not, have also given rise to troubles such as luxating patellae (slipping kneecaps). Many of the breeds with shortened legs such as the terriers (particularly the Yorkshire terrier) and others such as the miniature poodle are extremely prone to this phenomenon. The reasons for luxation have not been clearly defined and probably involve a number of factors. The most likely to play an early role is a malalignment of the major muscles and bones in the leg. The large group of muscles called the quadriceps on the front of the thigh is attached to the top of the tibia by a tendon in which the kneecap sits. These muscles are extremely strong and act to straighten the leg from a bent position. If the legs are slightly bowed this massive muscle group will effectively be trying to pull the kneecap out of the groove it sits in. In many of these breeds, probably as a result of inherited defects, this groove has become shallow or non-existent and so the muscles can pull the kneecap out of place almost constantly. It is also thought that in a circular way the pull of these muscle groups in young animals with bowed legs can deform the legs even more because the abnormal strains on the growth plates in the bones further distort the way they grow. There is a wide range of severity but nearly all require surgical intervention and nearly all will develop arthritis prematurely because of the joint instability and incongruity.

I once encountered an eight-week-old Yorkie puppy that came in for its first vaccination. The owners placed the dog and its sister on the table and it was immediately apparent that the male had something very wrong with him. He walked with his back legs completely straight and his spine had already become curved in an attempt to compensate for his dysfunctional back legs. I mentioned it to the owners and they said they had thought he wasn't quite right. They also told me that when they had gone to see the puppies the breeder had let all the other puppies run around on the floor but had handed this one straight to them to hold. Now being the cynic that I am, I assumed that the breeder had noticed the deformity, which was quite striking, and was trying to fob them off. I may be wrong. On examination I found that the back legs would not bend at all so I said we would have to X-ray him. I sent the X-rays to an orthopaedic specialist to make sure I gave the owners the right advice. The report showed that the legs were so deformed that the patellae were so permanently luxated and small that they sat at the back of the knee. The dog was euthanased. Putting young animals to sleep is the worst part of my job. It is such a waste and in cases like this it is even more galling because it is so unnecessary.

Wrinkles and Skin Folds

Another feature that usually goes hand in hand with short legs and indeed short faces is skin folds. What people fail to realise is that if you shorten a bone over time the skin does not automatically shorten with it. Therefore you have the same amount of skin but just bunched up like a wrinkled sock. Now strangely, skin folds are something that people find cute. You see a poster of a wrinkly boxer or bulldog puppy or, even worse, a Shar Pei and everyone starts swooning over how cute they are. It is not until you have seen the horribly inflamed and chronically infected skin that sits in between these folds that you start to revise your opinion. Skin is not designed to be permanently folded. You will not find examples of it anywhere in nature. Yes, rhinos and elephants have heavy wrinkles but these open up as the animal moves and their skin is not covered in fur. In humans that are extremely obese we see the same infected folds in between the rolls of fat. I'm sure anyone that has suffered with it will tell you how unpleasant it is.

Our skin and that of all animals is an amazing organ. It can clean itself, it is waterproof and it supports an incredible number of bacteria. These bacteria in general are in balance. They live in their own little micro-climate and, as long as the skin remains unbroken, don't usually cause any problems. When you fold a piece of skin you alter that climate. You make it warm and moist and you stop the air getting to it. This causes some bacteria to die and it lets a lot of other bacteria grow and reproduce in vast numbers. The constant moisture starts to soften and weaken the skin and then bacteria start to get into the top layers and the body mounts a response to try to kill them. This is inflammation. The skin becomes inflamed, infected and intensely itchy and red. Dogs with skin-fold pyoderma (skin infection) are depressing cases. They often need repeated courses of antibiotics and they very rarely get better without surgical removal of the offending folds. Some people joke

94

about these dogs having to have 'facelifts'. While it may be humorous to mock the latest celebrity that has gone under the knife for the sake of vanity, having to give dogs anaesthetics and surgery simply to make life bearable doesn't seem very funny to me.

With this in mind you can imagine my surprise when I discovered that the Kennel Club book tells me that pronounced wrinkles are highly desirable, if not essential in no less than sixteen breeds. This doesn't even include many of the short-faced breeds such as the Cavalier, Lhasa Apso and other such dogs that have skin folds secondary to their 'desirable' short muzzle.

Apart from the infections of the folds, wrinkles can have other effects. I recently had to operate on a very sweet young pug called Wat Tyler because his eyes were constantly being scratched by his eyelashes. Anyone that has had a hair in their eye for more than a few seconds will appreciate the discomfort this dog had been in for months. The large folds of skin on his ridiculously short face were causing his eyelids to roll inwards. The standard for this breed states that the face should have 'wrinkles clearly defined'. His eye condition is called entropion. Usually the only option for

Wat Tyler, bright-eyed after entropion surgery.

© Emma Milne

95

these dogs is surgery. If left, you get recurrent ulcers on the surface of the eye, pain and potentially a perforated ulcer leading to the loss of the eye. I am happy to say that Wat has made a good and speedy recovery and looks a lot more comfortable now.

In fact, before I went to university I spent some time, as I said, at a practice in Maidstone. There was a young, newly-qualified vet working there at the time and we got on very well. She was everything I wanted to be. I watched her perform the exact same operation on a Shar Pei. During the operation the dog stopped breathing, and despite extremely intensive efforts to resuscitate it the dog died. The vet was understandably mortified and went to phone the owner. The owner was obviously upset and became semi-hysterical on the phone. The young dog had cost her around £2,000 as a puppy. She demanded an independent post-mortem and the dog was taken to a neighbouring practice. They discovered that the dog had a deformed heart and would probably not have reached maturity. This experience will stay with me for a long time. The vet had gone through what every vet fears the most – losing a patient. The dog was so inbred that it may not even have survived, but it had had to have surgery that could have been completely prevented if it wasn't 'supposed' to have 'loose skin' and a 'frowning expression'.

My husband, some months ago, was brought a rescue Neapolitan mastiff by the local branch of the RSPCA. The dog had been homed from the breeder only to be returned at an early age due to chronic eye disease. The dog had ended up at the RSPCA near us at the age of about five months. The breed standard for this dog requires 'a degree of loose fitting skin over body and head'. These features in many of the typically droopy-eyed breeds such as the mastiff, bloodhound, Clumber spaniel, chow chow and bulldog, to name but a few, contribute to a condition called 'diamond eye'. The diamond shape of the eye has some areas of eyelid that turn inwards, as in the previous case of the pug, making the lashes constantly rub the eye and parts of the lids fall away. The eye is then very susceptible to trauma, inflammation and pain.

This young mastiff had so much loose skin that the resulting diamond eye had already caused irreversible damage to one of his eyes and chronic ulceration of the other. He had one eye removed at six months and had to have approximately six inches of skin removed from the top of his head to try to address the excessive

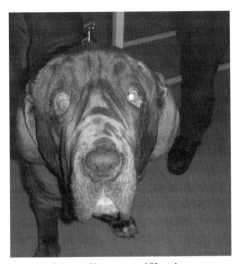

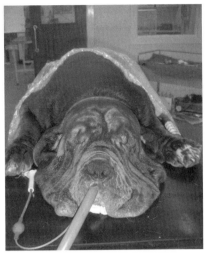

Neapolitan mastiff prior
to eye and skin removal.
© Mark Goodman

Neapolitan mastiff at the time of
surgery.
© Mark Goodman

folds of skin and save his other eye. He is now thankfully with a loving family but a big dog with these diseases is never going to be an easy or cheap treatment option, never mind the fact that such a young animal is suffering unnecessarily.

The same rescue centre now has two Shar Peis that have both

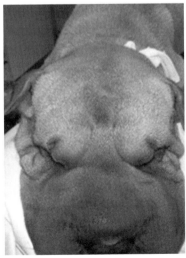

Buster prior to entropion surgery.
© Tanya Banks

Buster under general anaesthetic.
© Mark Goodman

Buster after surgery enjoying a cuddle from his friend Millie.
© Tanya Banks

had to have skin-reduction operations, entropion correction and ear surgery. One of them is also very aggressive, making it very unlikely he will ever find a home. One of our neighbours and good friends was bought a Shar Pei puppy by a boyfriend as a present. He is a very sweet dog and seeing him play with his good friend William the greyhound is lovely to see. Unfortunately but inevitably we have already been asked to look at his constantly watering eyes. In a sitting position his eyes were almost not visible because of the weight of the skin that was rolling his eyelids down onto the surface of his eyes. We really had no option but to operate. His mum tells us that since the surgery his quality of life and also his confidence has greatly improved. After all, he is now pain-free and can actually see.

Although the breed standard now says, 'any sign of irritation of eyeball, conjunctiva or eyelids highly undesirable' (fairly obvious to most I would have thought), I have to wonder whether this is actually wishful thinking. The breed is still relatively uncommon here but every one I've seen or heard about has had problems. The introductory information in the Kennel Club book also tells

A Shar Pei puppy with very severe entropion due to skin folds.
© Dr David Gould

us that the 'early specimens from America tended to give a very unfortunate impression'. It goes on to say that they 'suffered almost 100% from entropion ... necessitating frequent veterinary attention'. It then suggests that this has been properly addressed now by breeders and they now enjoy 'better fitting skin and better eyelids'. Based on what I've seen I'm not convinced!

I will furnish you with one more example from the Kennel Club standards, this time for the bloodhound. These dogs have been famous for years because of their ability to do their job. They obviously have an incredible sense of smell and a great tracking ability. Surely for such a dog this should be the overriding thing we look for in a good example of the breed. Nowadays according to the standard they should have, 'head furnished with an amount of loose skin, which in nearly every position appears abundant, but more particularly so when the head is carried low; skin then falls into loose, pendulous ridges and folds, especially over the forehead and sides of the face.' This is actually saying the folds will, and should be, much more pronounced when the head is low, i.e. when the dog is working on a scent.

This breed and many of the others I am highlighting are cause for concern as far as the European Convention on Pet Animals is concerned and, I believe, should be cause for concern for all of us. We'll look at the convention and what it proposes later.

I have not encountered many bassets in my time but almost all of them have had skin disease in their folds. In fact I had one client whose basset was so distressed all the time that she was considering having her put to sleep. These skin diseases are lifelong unless surgically treated but in the case of most dogs the wrinkling is so extensive that intervention would be impossible.

As I have said skin folds can cause a big problem in many ways, either by becoming inflamed and infected or simply by affecting surrounding structures such as the globe of the eye. However, we see a massive amount of skin disease in general. Bassets do not only have skin disease from folds of skin but are also prone to other types of skin disorder. Many of these diseases we see in breeds such as the basset and the West Highland white arise from a number of causes but probably have an inherited factor in some cases. I always remember a lecturer at university telling us that skin disease is often both miserable for the dog and lucrative for the vet. They rarely get better, they rarely kill the animal and they often require lifelong medication and treatment. I now see his point. Skin disorders such as allergies, atopy and seborrhoea, in which the skin becomes very greasy and smelly, are not pleasant for animal or owner. Many bassets have a combination of skin diseases as well as other problems.

You will start to notice as we go through the body and the body systems that some breed names will crop up time and again. It is these breeds that I believe we should be standing back from and taking a look at. I hope you will see that I am not just trying to be controversial with this information. I am trying to raise a genuine point and issue of animal welfare. We are so quick to judge other countries for their intensive farming or their whaling and so on, but we – supposedly a nation of animal lovers – have a real problem here ourselves.

Big Ears

Now, with my history I am hardly going to start criticising those with large ears! Sadly this is no laughing matter. The truth is that many breeds have been bred to have ears that are heavy, hairy, long, thick and all variations in between. Wolves have upright, pricked, open ears. This allows them to hear extremely well and locate the source of a sound. The movement of the ears is also used as a form of communication. When flattened they indicate submission and when raised show confidence. The insides of their ear canals are relatively fur-free and air can easily circulate. The canals are open allowing wax and debris from the canal to be expelled.

I'm sure you can see where I'm going with this. Because of our desire for variations in ear shape and conformation we have taken a well-designed organ and made it malfunction. Although the actual hearing may not be directly affected there are many consequences of abnormal ear shape. I will give you some examples.

Basset hounds are an obvious choice. The ears 'should' be 'Set on low, just below line of eye. Long; reaching well beyond end of muzzle of correct length, but not excessively so.' I'm not sure I understand this correctly. How can an ear that is to reach well beyond the length of the muzzle not be considered excessive? These dogs have ears that are so long and heavy they actually trail on the floor and in their food. They are often encrusted with dinner remains and are exposed to injury. The weight of the ear stops air getting into the canal and wax and so on getting out. The canal will be moist and warm and start to resemble all their other skin folds. Chronic infections are commonplace and sometimes, once again, surgical intervention may be necessary.

The nature of these ears also makes any surgery that's required more difficult. The ears have to be bandaged up on top of the head or 'pegged' together somehow. People think it very humorous post-operatively, but surgically they can be a nightmare. Bloodhounds have similar ears that 'should' be '... long, set low and falling in graceful folds...'

Spaniels such as the springer and the cocker have very heavy, hairy ears and canals. I have spent numerous summers fishing grass seeds and twigs out of spaniels' ear canals. It seems strange that we are very happy to amputate their tails in case of injury but yet their ears should be 'lobular', 'extending to nose tip', 'large', 'nicely feathered', 'thick' and 'set low', depending on what particular spaniel they are.

We recently dog-sat for our friend's working springer, Henry. He is a very sweet dog with not a bad bone in his body and likes to think he is attached to you by a small piece of elastic that does not allow him to be further than a foot away from you at any time. We went to the woods with 'the boys', where they love to be, and had our usual hour-long walk. Henry had a great time. He was doing what spaniels do best: rummaging and foraging around and generally tearing about like the proverbial headless chicken. His nose was glued to the floor. What astounded me was that his ears trailed constantly on the floor. We got back and they were absolutely covered in sticky buds and all sorts of woodland debris. I know our friend spends lots of time after every walk picking things out of Henry's ears and the covering fur but I can't believe that large shooting estates can have the time to devote to this for their dogs. I know people love spaniels and they are a very nice type of dog, but surely some owners must admit that maybe it would be nice if their ears were just a bit *smaller*?

Poodles, among other such breeds, have ear canals that are absolutely stuffed full of hair. This has the effect of reducing air flow and of trapping all the normal secretions of the ear lining in the canal. Again, chronic irritation and infection are commonplace. Poodles often have their ears plucked while at the grooming parlour. For those of you with that middle-aged phenomenon of hair in your ears, try pulling it out with tweezers and see what it feels like, then imagine hair extending right to your eardrum and see whether you would relish letting someone remove it by plucking!

As I said with skin disease, ear disease often arises out of a number of factors. Long gone are the days of saying dogs had 'canker'. In years gone by, ear disease was viewed mostly as an entity separate to the rest of the skin. Nowadays, however, we know that ear and skin disease are inextricably linked. After all, ears are covered in skin. Many breeds such as the basset, retriever, Labrador, Westie and poodle are prone to chronic ear disease, partly because of conformation in some cases and partly because of inherited or predisposed disease. My daylist every summer is full of these dogs that are shaking their heads, scratching their ears and often traumatised because of the discomfort. Ask any vet what the most distinctive smells of our career are and somewhere on most people's list among the infected teeth, the anal glands and the rotting placentas will be that grim, waxy, greasy smell that emanates from many of these dogs.

Squashed Faces

The definition of the word 'brachycephalic' is 'having a short, wide head'. The breeds that would fall into this category are ones such as the boxer, bulldog, pug, Pekinese, Japanese Chin, cavalier King Charles spaniel and shih-tzu. One example of the standard is for the Pekinese. It states that the head should be large and 'proportionately wider than deep'. The Kennel Club book also enlightens us that the breed 'is not the long country walk type' and although 'strong and heavy for his size, he is, however, easy to tuck under an arm and take anywhere'. How convenient!

As we have bred these dogs to have shorter and shorter faces, until in some cases they start to look like they have run at speed into a brick wall, there are several things that have happened as a consequence. As with the bones of the leg where the soft tissue gets left behind the same happens with the soft tissue of the face and mouth. The problem is that this is potentially a lot more serious than having some loose skin hanging round your ankles. These breeds often encounter a number of problems, which added together, account for 'brachycephalic syndrome'. That's right – we have a whole syndrome of problems that these dogs have to endure to meet the breed standards. Indeed, Gough and Thomas describe the syndrome as a complex of anatomical deformities and a 'likely consequence of selective breeding for certain facial characteristics'.

The most apparent sign of this syndrome will be obvious to anyone that has looked lovingly at their partner with the dog asleep at their feet and smiled at each other as the dog snores its head off in that cute way. There is a good reason that these dogs snore and it is the reason that makes them intolerant of extremes of exercise, causes them to pant almost continuously and makes them a higher risk for anaesthesia.

The best way to approach this will be to start at the nose and work our way down the respiratory tract. The first place we encounter a problem is straight away at the nose. Brachycephalic breeds are prone to what we call stenotic nares. This means that the nostril holes are very small and thus do not allow much passage of air. This is one reason why many of these dogs pant almost constantly because they simply cannot shift enough air through the nasal passages to get sufficient oxygen. Some dogs that have the worst cases of this do require surgery to open up the nostrils.

As you move backwards through the mouth the next thing you encounter is the tongue. In these dogs the tongue is often very large relative to the mouth because the mouth is so short. The tongue, particularly in the larger breeds is very large and thick and tends to protrude a lot of the time. In the smaller breeds they tend to curl up out of the mouth. In one of the practices I used to work in we had a couple who had taken on a runt bulldog. Now, in fairness, I honestly believe these people thought they were doing the right thing by giving a loving home to an unwanted dog. This dog had the most twisted and bowed front legs I have ever seen and the couple had to carry him most of the time, presumably because walking was a struggle. I used to see him primarily because he had chronic ear disease. He was prone to infections caused by a bacterium called Pseudomonas. Anyone in a medical profession will know that this bacterium is incredibly resistant to many antibiotics and there are only a few left at our disposal with which to treat it. This has raised many concerns about the over-use of these drugs in case we end up with nothing that will work. The truth is that I was revolted every time I saw this poor little dog. His jaw was so short and deformed that half of the length of his tongue physically didn't fit in his mouth. The half that didn't hung permanently like a piece of dried leather from his mouth. His breathing was atrocious. Now, with all the best intentions I believe in my heart of hearts that this dog should have been put to sleep. I believe that his quality of life was not what we should expect for an animal. He was a very extreme case but many of these dogs do struggle to one degree or another.

Moving back you reach the soft palate. This is the division between the nasal pharynx and the oral pharynx; that is, the cavities at the back of the mouth. In these breeds the palate tends to be too long and gets sucked in and out of the windpipe. This is one reason the dogs snore and why they struggle to exercise hard. Many dogs every year have to undergo surgery to trim the palate to stop the obstruction of the trachea or windpipe.

Finally we come to the trachea itself. The windpipe, as it is more commonly known, is obviously a pretty important structure to have functional. In 'normal' animals it is wide and strong and is capable of not only allowing sufficient air to pass through it at times of extreme exercise but it can cope with a wide range of air pressures as well. Brachycephalic animals can have what is called a 'hypoplastic' trachea. This simply means it has not grown as much as one would expect. In effect these tracheas can be incredibly narrow and simply cannot meet the demands of air supply that are needed during exercise. Hypoplastic tracheas are the equivalent of having to breathe through a straw the whole time.

Another consequence of the shortened jaw is that there is no longer enough room for the teeth to sit in a normal position. This has meant that the sockets have had to twist in their positions in order to be accommodated. In some cases some teeth have disappeared altogether. Another trait that goes hand in hand with these breeds is an undershot jaw. This is where the bottom jaw sticks out beyond the top. These dogs' teeth do not line up as they are intended to do and it can cause problems in some cases because the teeth impinge on the gums and other tissues. In the most extreme cases the dogs can have difficulty picking food up because the teeth are so far out of line. This would be seen as a fault in any 'normal' animal. In fact, while looking through the Kennel Club book I have found twelve breeds in which it is considered acceptable or desirable to be undershot. Examples of these are the pug ('slightly undershot'), the Boston terrier ('bite even, or sufficiently undershot to square muzzle'), the French bulldog ('slightly undershot') and so on.

It is not just at times of stress and exercise that these animals are at danger. In the surgery they can present a problem. When animals are anaesthetised we place a tube into the trachea to supply anaesthetic gas and oxygen. All anaesthetics suppress the circulation and respiration to some degree or another. These breeds of dog tend to be harder to tube because of the excess soft tissue in the mouth and pharynx and the narrow tracheas. Also, in recovery when the tube is removed, they are at a much higher risk of post-operative complications because the airways are so occluded by soft tissue. We often have to prop the mouth open with some type of hollow roll such as a bandage roll to allow normal respiration

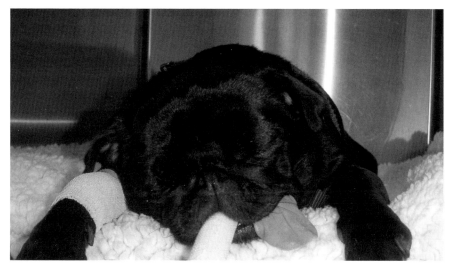
Pug in recovery after general anaesthetic.
© Mark Goodman

until the animal is conscious enough to resume its 'normal' (in the loosest sense of the word) breathing.

As I said earlier I am a fan of films and another quote often springs to mind during my daily encounters with some of these dogs. I don't mean this in an irreverent way; these things just pop into my head just the same as *Monty Python's Holy Grail* will always come into my head every time I see 'a duck!' I am referring to the film *Ghostbusters*, which surely all will agree is a classic of the 80s. There is a point after they have just set up the business and are struggling and one of the busters is upset that they have no clients and takes it out on the receptionist and points out her rather bulbous eyes. As he storms past the desk after the insult he obviously feels remorse at the comment and calls over his shoulder, 'Sorry about the bug-eyes thing.' This makes me smile every single time I think about it. This is fairly frequent because I think about it every time I see a pug or a Pekinese or, these days, a Cavalier King Charles spaniel. The smile soon disappears when I see the trouble that 'bug-eyes' give our dogs.

Bulbous eyes are much more prone to injury not just because they protrude but because of the nasal and facial folds of skin that so often go hand in hand with these eyes. I was looking at some pug sites on the internet because I was trying to remember which

A Pekinese with extremely bulging eyes due to shallow sockets.
© Dr David Gould

famous historical character Edwina, whom I mentioned earlier, had told me loved pugs and I came across this absolutely classic quote from an interview with various women involved with pug breeding and showing for many years:

'This dog is wonderful around children, but kids can be rough and they can easily damage a pug's eyes,' she says. Some experts even warn about the presence of cats and suggest that any pointy or dangerous objects lying around be removed or they could inadvertently poke the large exposed surface of a pug's eye. As for the theory that pugs' eyes pop out, 'Absolute nonsense,' claims Kerry. 'Pugs' eyes are bulbous so it could be easier for their eyes to pop out than those of some other breeds, but the dog would have to be grabbed by another dog for it to happen. In all my time connected with this breed, I have only known of two dogs whose eyes have popped out. Unlike some other breeds, such as the King Charles Spaniel, this problem is not prevalent in the Pug.'

What a healthy breed they must be! My word, only two with eyes that have inadvertently *fallen out*! Come on, guys, I'm tearing my hair out here. I'm not the only one that thinks that's a bit mad, am I? Can you imagine a wild animal having evolved with eyes that were so bulging that they fell out?

108

A pug with extremely bulging eyes due to shallow sockets.
© Dr David Gould

This same woman actually goes on to say, on the subject we were discussing earlier:

> Can one lose sleep if bombarded nightly by the famous Pug snore? 'They do snore, but so do old people,' laughs Kerry. She stresses that the breed does not have a breathing problem and is perfectly healthy if looked after properly. 'Sometimes you can hear a Pug panting away, but that's often caused by heat, which causes stress, making the dog pant. It's not a breathing problem.'

This oft-heard comment by lovers of such brachycephalic breeds not only makes me very angry, it is actually an incredibly misleading thing to say. As I said, how are the public to have any inkling that a breed may have health concerns when such rubbish is spoken by the 'experts' on the breeds who are in apparently total denial about these problems. Heat makes all dogs pant, that is how they control their body temperature. In these breeds, to varying degrees, their ability to exchange air enough to pant or cope with the lowest levels of stress is severely compromised. This *is* in fact a breathing problem.

I had another dear client in Cheltenham who had a similar love of 'Pekes'. She had similar views to Edwina. Her father had bought her a Peke as a birthday present when she was a girl and since

109

then she had always had them. Like Edwina she now only takes on rescues because she thinks the changes in the breed have gone too far. I say again, these are lovely dogs, I have nothing against them; it isn't their fault that they have been 'devolved'. Sophie used to come in fairly frequently to have her nails trimmed (this is the dog I'm talking about now, not her owner!). She also had only one eye, the other being lost through injury. Sophie didn't like having her nails cut and her owner, bless her, didn't like to watch so would always leave the room. Julie, the nurse, would hold Sophie for me. At the slightest restraint Sophie would not only start to struggle for air because of her brachycephalic airways but her remaining eye would bulge dangerously close to the rim of its socket and we always worried that it would actually fall out.

Sophie the one-eyed Peke.
© Emma Milne

I was talking to Mark about it one night and he said that he had actually seen a Peke's eye fall out while being restrained for an anaesthetic. This *isn't* something we should be unsurprised by! Do you know how hard it would be to increase the cranial pressure of a 'normal' dog enough to get its eyes to fall out? Nigh on impossible.

Last year I went on a week-long course on ophthalmology (still making up for my deficiencies at university) and neurology. The speakers were both esteemed specialists in their field. I got talking to them one evening after lectures had finished. Cavalier spaniels had been mentioned during the lecture and I wanted to ask about their 'squint'. I know breeders will say it is not a squint, but having football eyes (one's at home and one's away) isn't usually considered normal in a dog. The neurologist made the point that Cavaliers' skulls have been deformed and made smaller so much over the years that the eyes don't actually fit in the skull anymore. Incredible.

Another problem that is coming more to the fore at the moment in this breed is a condition called syringomyelia. This condition has varying signs from none at all to scratching at the ears or neck to severe pain and neurological deficits. It is the development of cavities in the spinal cord in the neck. These cavities occur because the flow of the fluid round the spine and in the brain is obstructed. This can be for a number of reasons but in some small breeds and particularly the Cavalier it is because the skull is too small to house the back of the brain. This area called the cerebellum then gets herniated out of the back of the skull and blocks the flow of fluid.

Clare Rusbridge, a European specialist in veterinary neurology, has been working with some breeders over the last couple of years and has started a screening programme. This is done using MRI scanning. The fact is that because some of these dogs are asymptomatic MRI scanning is the only way to know for sure if it is present and avoid breeding from affected animals. It is thought that the prevalence in Cavaliers could be as high as 50 per cent. An article in the *Vet Times* in July 2006 said that, 'a lot of breeders don't agree with the scan'. Surely anyone with the welfare of the breed at heart would embrace this unreservedly. Wouldn't they?

Hairy Monsters and Dumb Animals

We have also bred a large number of dogs that have very long coats. Long coats can be quite overwhelming in our brief summers. Every year I see so many dogs that come in and are panting like mad with a huge fur coat on. Dogs can't sweat through their skin the way we can. They have some sweat glands on the pads but they rely on panting for the majority of their cooling requirements. I for one can't imagine what this must be like but I think it must be akin to us being fully clothed in winter clothes and going somewhere where the humidity is 100 per cent and there is no breeze. It must be awful. I know some breeds are traditionally clipped, but many aren't and this doesn't mean they *can't* be. Breeds like collies and retrievers and even shepherds would benefit massively from being clipped in the summer.

About four or five years ago in summer I realised how much Pan was struggling in the heat. We were at our beloved Crickley Hill and it was a very hot day. Pan was walking next to me like an old dog, which was very unusual for him. Unlike Badger he has an incredibly dense and woolly undercoat. I took him to the surgery and set about him with a pair of clippers. Now, I am no groomer, had no clipper guards and to be frank I made an awful job of it. At one point Pan looked round at himself and sighed deeply and adopted an Eeyore pose of deep resignation. By the time I had finished he was surrounded by enough fur to make two more dogs and had completely changed colour because his undercoat is very light grey as opposed to his usual black. The general consensus among the others at work was that Pan would be the laughing stock of his doggy friends. Regardless of all this I took him back to our favourite hill that same afternoon and he ran about like a puppy. He was literally a different dog. Now every summer he is clipped as often as he needs doing.

I met a very nice man at the beach recently who was the proud

112

owner of a clipped Border collie. We got talking as dog owners often do. We were extolling the virtues of the clipped dog, not least because of the reduction in fur to be hoovered up at home. He commented that when he had told his sister that he intended to clip the dog she had told him he simply couldn't because collies aren't normally clipped. This is a really common scenario. Why should it matter if they are usually clipped or not? When I go out on a hot day I don't wear all my winter clothes so why do we expect our dogs to do the same?

A very dear and long-standing client of mine used to have a sheltie called Duke. Duke developed heart failure as he got older and started struggling with his respiration. He responded well to medication but obviously there is only so much the drugs can do. I saw him one day in the summer and Duke was heaving and panting. I suggested to Chris that he take Duke to the groomers and have him clipped. I also told him to make sure they really 'buzzed' him. I saw them both the following week for a check-up and couldn't help laughing as I had done with Pan. He looked totally different and we both had a chuckle over the new, slim-line Duke. Anyway, it helped him enormously and took one more strain off his heart.

Mark also often suggests clipping to his clients since seeing the difference it makes to Pan. He recently had a client in with two shelties and he had suggested having them clipped. The owner declined on the grounds that 'it would take all year to grow back'. Who cares? The point is that your dog really has no concept of how bad its haircut is or how different it looks. It will, however, experience the enormous relief that we get when we peel off layers of clothes when we are sweating like a pig.

Many dogs with long fur have their vision obscured by their fur or end up having to go through the indignity of having bows put in their hair to keep it out of their eyes. I've seen many a dog that constantly licked their lips and mouth because they always had fur in there. Many 'bearded' dogs have saliva staining all round the mouth and you can often smell the fur in that area because it is harbouring all manner of decaying food. If you picture any wild animal, particularly carnivores, you will struggle to come up with one that has long fur round its mouth. Imagine a leopard or a hyena pushing its head into a bloody carcass as it gorges on its prey. Short hair on the muzzle is essential for hygiene and I'm sure many owners of bearded dogs would find them much more pleasant when the chin is rested so endearingly on the knee if they didn't leave behind a trail of slime and last night's dinner.

The distressing thing about all of this is that we have created these dogs for their looks and seem unwilling to consider the welfare of the animal for the sake of the breed standard. I have wracked my brain long and hard and can think of no animals in the wild that naturally have extremely long fur. It seems to me that such a characteristic in the wild would be more of a hindrance than a help and would attract an awful lot of knots, twigs and other assorted debris. Long fur would not evolve for warmth because nature's way of dealing with the cold is either very dense, but short fur or a thick layer of fat.

When we do clip dogs there are many breeds that have it dictated which bits should be clipped. How many dogs do you see such as the schnauzer that have their bodies clipped but the most annoying fur over their eyes and round their mouth left long? The cocker spaniel and Westies to name a couple have the top of the body clipped and a hovercraft-style skirt left behind that must be a nightmare on walks. The ornamental clipping of poodles leaves me speechless. Indeed, the Kennel Club book states that, 'for the fashion-conscious there are many different styles in which he can be clipped. A dandy at heart, he will always show his appreciation when his toilette has been completed.' Please, if you want a doll there are plenty available in most good toyshops.

Show types of breeds such as the Yorkie, Skye terrier, Hungarian puli, Komondor, Afghan and Old English sheepdog for the show ring require extremely long fur. These extreme lengths of fur are totally artificial and would never exist in nature. All these dogs would be much happier and cooler with short, manageable fur and I'm sure they wouldn't be too upset at the fact that they don't qualify for the Timotei adverts any more.

You may be wondering why the chapter title mentions dumb animals and I will tell you. I realise that this is not a very politically correct way of describing those that can't talk anymore but I hope you will allow me a little poetic licence.

One of the consequences that even fewer people consider with all these aberrations is the effect it has on the ability of our dogs to communicate with each other. Dogs display a large number of signals that express their mood and whether they are feeling confident or aggressive or submissive. A confident dog will stand very erect, prick up its ears and hold its tail erect. A submissive dog will flatten its ears, cower and have its tail down. A threatened dog will raise its hackles. I'm sure you can see where I'm going with this. Eye contact, or lack of it, is also very important.

Dogs that have very long, heavy ears cannot effectively display confidence; very shaggy dogs cannot raise their hackles and dogs without tails can do very little to communicate at all. I was recently talking to a very good behavioural specialist and I asked him if he encountered many behavioural problems in docked dogs. He said that, yes, he did see some but the worst for him was the Old English sheepdog. I had never really considered this before but could immediately see what he meant. These dogs' faces, lips and ears are covered in hair, they cannot effectively raise their hackles, they cannot make or avoid eye contact and 99 per cent of them have been docked. We have effectively made these dogs mute. Dogs that cannot communicate can have problems in that they draw aggression from other dogs because the other dogs are unsure about how to approach the meeting. This really is not in the best interests of the animal, which leads me very nicely onto the subject of tail-docking.

Tail-Docking

Caffreys; a beautiful boxer as nature intended.
© Mr and Mrs Carmichael

Many of you will already be aware of my views on the subject of tail-docking so I apologise for going over old ground and flogging what must be now a rapidly dying horse. For those of you who are uninitiated you will either be angered or enlightened, but you will also hopefully start to look at dogs in a whole different way.

Big advances have been made recently with regard to this subject. I still feel it is worth looking at what exactly it is and why some people believe it should go on before we examine the current state of play.

For those of you that don't know, tail-docking is when the tail of a puppy is removed between one and five days of age (although I know personally of one vet who carried it out at eight days of age because the breeder had been too busy and had forgotten to

116

get it done). The tails are usually either cut off with scissors or a scalpel or have a rubber band placed round them until the dead bit falls off. Now you will be told that, when carried out properly, this is a completely painless procedure. Indeed, the Council for Docked Breeds (CDB) maintains that some puppies docked while they are asleep will not even wake up. Let me ask you this – can you imagine a human baby peacefully sleeping through someone cutting off its little finger with a pair of scissors? Try putting a rubber band on the end of your finger and see how long it takes before the pain starts and then see how long you can stand it. I have personally spoken to many people, mostly unwilling nurses forced to hold the puppies, who have seen the procedure. I have yet to meet someone who was not sickened. I know that more than one of them threatened to resign if she was ever involved again.

The fact is that the majority of people in this country, when informed about the practice, are against the procedure, and it is, in fact, only a small minority of showers and breeders that want it to continue. In my opinion the Kennel Club is largely to blame for the fact that it has not been stopped. On past questioning the Kennel Club have repeatedly said that they must be governed by the laws of the land and therefore cannot do anything about it all the time it is legal. However, if the Club were actually opposed to the practice they could have stopped it practically overnight by not allowing docked animals to be shown. As we will see, this may well be the case from now on.

The fact is that there is still a massive amount of ignorance about it. I don't mean this in an offensive way. How can we expect the public to know the truth when the people who are docking these animals are so underhand about it? I was told recently of someone who had been informed by a breeder of Jack Russells that 70 per cent of them are born without tails now because they have been docked for so many years. This is a genetic impossibility and is typical of the rubbish that is spoken by some of these people.

So, let's look at what the Council for Docked Breeds (CDB) says. Let's take each of their reasons for docking one by one and see what we think. It's not rocket science to pick them apart because not one of them has any logic behind it.

1. To avoid tail damage
This is their favourite one. Many breeds of dogs have traditionally

been docked to prevent tail damage later in life. Typically these have been working breeds such as spaniels and pointers. Apparently their 'enthusiastic' tail action causes them untold misery and injury when they work. The CDB even goes on to suggest that for some dogs this injury can even happen in the home to non-working breeds.

Where do I begin? I have received lots of correspondence from owners of working undocked dogs that have never had a problem in their lives. Why have spaniels been bred to have long, floppy, hairy ears when surely this is the first point of contact they have with gorse and brambles? I have seen it many times. I have pulled many grass seeds and pieces of twig out of spaniel ears and feet. These procedures invariably require sedation or full general anaesthesia but I don't hear anyone advocating ear-cropping for the breed.

During the tail-docking debate for the new Animal Welfare Bill I heard many pro-dock people saying that if dogs had to be docked later in life due to injury they would have to undergo an anaesthetic and a prolonged and painful recovery. This is hypocritical nonsense. First, they don't seem to be so concerned about the anaesthesia required for grass seed removal. Second, any surgical procedure these days should be pain-free due to the standard use of analgesics and, third, within a week to ten days the tail is healed. If dogs aren't allowed sufficient time off work to recover from any surgery it surely is a cause for concern.

One breed we see very commonly used for working is the Labrador. Labradors have an incredibly 'waggy' tail and we do sometimes see a condition called 'Labrador tail'. This is where the dog loses the ability to lift or move the tail and it can be quite painful. It is generally considered to be fatigue from a day of strenuous wagging. Surely docking would prevent this terrible suffering? Oh no, that's right Labradors aren't 'traditionally' docked.

In the case of pointers I am even more at a loss. The English pointer is undocked but the German pointer is docked. Even more odd is that the German shorthaired pointer is docked but the German longhaired pointer is not! Why on earth are fox hounds not docked? The most important point to make here is that, as outlined by the RCVS, it is impossible to know at one to five days of age which dogs will be workers and which will be pets and the injury argument

118

is therefore not a valid reason for docking. Presumably many of the terrier breeds were originally docked because of their work. Let me ask you this: when was the last time you saw a working Yorkshire terrier? Besides the terriers when was the last time you saw a *poodle* work?

As for non-working breeds, the injury argument reaches a new level of ridiculousness. Over the years I have had to amputate many tails either fully or partially through chronic, unhealing injury or trauma. Among the dogs these have been staffies, a couple of Labradors but most often greyhounds. Greyhounds are kennelled a lot of the time either in racing kennels or, unfortunately and all too commonly, in rescue centres once they have served their purpose to the race industry. Their tails are long and whiplike, and covered in particularly thin skin. Not a single pro-docker is suggesting they should be routinely docked. We'll see why in a moment. But by far the highest number of tails I have amputated have been those of cats. They get run over, they get trapped in doors or underfoot, they get injured in fights and so on and so on. No one advocates the docking of cats' tails. Well, they use them for communication and balance, don't they? H'm, sounds familiar.

My two dogs also have an enthusiastic tail action. We have developed amazing reflexes for grabbing glasses off the coffee table when one of them walks past it. They have never hurt their tails. Should I dock them on the off-chance or for my own convenience? I was walking my dogs today and I saw a family coming towards me. I couldn't see any dogs at first and then three beautiful springers came tearing out of the bushes. Every one of them had a long, glorious tail and it made my day. They looked *so* happy. It was a joy to see. That got me thinking about the whole issue, as it does every time I see a docked dog or one that 'should' be but isn't. I started thinking about the argument I have just made about avoiding all injuries. It occurred to me that I should say something along the lines of: 'What if we kept all dogs indoors for a year? We would see no fight wounds, no cut pads, no grass seeds and no lameness.' It then occurred to me that that situation has already happened to a lesser degree. During the foot-and-mouth outbreak people couldn't exercise their dogs anywhere near as much as they would usually. The surgery in which I was working at the time was practically empty. Farm work was booming but small-animal work dropped off noticeably. My point is proved. It is *easy* to stop

119

our dogs getting injured but it wouldn't be acceptable to say we should just keep them indoors. Therefore it is just as unacceptable to dock dogs routinely just in case they injure their tail in later life.

There is one totally fundamental point to make here which was never said in any of the debates I have heard on this issue. The people who wish to continue docking to prevent tail injury and amputation are inflicting the worst injury and performing the fullest amputations that tails can receive. With this in mind, if there was a total ban on all non-therapeutic docking you would be improving the welfare of every single dog that didn't injure its tail later in life. There are many estimates as to what this figure might be depending on which side of the fence you sit on. The very highest estimates suspect that approximately 1 in 100 dogs may injure their tails (and not all of these will require amputation) so banning docking could thus improve the welfare of well over 99% of dogs that would have been indiscriminately docked.

2. For reasons of hygiene

Another classic from the CDB. They suggest that long-haired dogs such as Yorkies and Old English sheepdogs should be docked because of the risk of faecal soiling, which could lead to flystrike and other serious health problems. I would suggest that anyone allowing this to happen should consider how well they have cared for their dog. If it is such a problem why not simply keep their rear ends clipped or breed for shorter coats? We've already seen that this would probably help many a dog in summer, if not all year round.

Why are other long-haired breeds such as bearded collies and rough collies not docked? German shepherds are well known for being predisposed to a condition called anal furunculosis, which is a potentially fatal, chronic, deep infection of the skin around the anus. There is a theory that it may be related to faecal soiling and the stiff hair of the tail constantly pushing the faeces into the skin. Why are they left with their tails? The Royal College states in its guidelines on professional conduct with regard to tail-docking that prevention of soiling is *not* considered just reason.

While we are on the subject, we may wonder why Persian cats aren't docked. All of this will soon become apparent when we look at reason three.

120

3. To maintain breed standards

This is my personal favourite and is obviously the major, only thinly disguised reason why tail-docking has continued to happen. It is worth looking closely at the CDB argument here so I will quote directly from their website:

> Breeds which have been docked over many generations have been selected for specific qualities of build and conformation, but not for tail length, shape or carriage. If left undocked, it is unlikely that the best dogs would carry good tails. In seeking to maintain the quality of the breeds, breeders would therefore be left with a diminished number of suitable sires and dams. The genetic pool would be reduced, greatly increasing the risk of hereditary diseases taking hold. Some breeds could even disappear for ever.

This honestly makes me laugh. I cannot believe that anyone would listen to such a load of tripe as this statement. How can a dog not have a 'good' tail? That is how they are born. The whole concept of the breed standard is an important cause of health problems and poor animal welfare in this country. The above statement by the CDB actually says that breeders will be so concerned with how their show dog looks that they will ignore the gene pool because they are 'forced' to select for 'good tails'. If they actually cared about their animals they would select for healthy, whole dogs that can lead a normal life.

The RCVS guide has long stated that docking for breed type or conformation is unethical and the veterinary surgeon involved can be struck off the register for professional misconduct. They use terms such as 'conduct *disgraceful* in a professional respect' and '*unacceptable mutilation*' (my italics). Are the CDB honestly saying they know more about the physiology and pain-receptors of these dogs than the governing body of the veterinary profession?

If docking has been illegal for lay-people since 1993 and is reason for being struck off for vets, why are there still so many dogs being docked? I know that many vets, my partner included, felt a sigh of relief when the law was changed in 1993. Everyone thought it would stop. I have had numerous emails from vets who have said that they have been battling against it for decades but all the time the surgery down the road keeps doing it how will it ever stop? The fact is that many vets kept doing it but nothing could be done about it because it couldn't be proved; the people who have the docking done are hardly going to report the vet and no records are kept. Ones who do get pulled up have extensive legal backing from the likes of the CDB and seem to keep getting away with it. We also come back to the same point as before here; as vets we invariably see puppies for the first time at eight to twelve weeks of age. The docking is done so early that by the time most prospective owners see the puppies they are already docked and no one thinks anything of it presumably because of the fact that 'that's how they're supposed to look'.

I often do mention it to new owners, though not in an accusatory way. I soon realised after talking to many owners that they simply had no idea about what went on or the reasons behind it. Most are horrified and will say they would have got a tailed one had they known. I recently met a new client under very sad circumstances. He is a loving owner and has had boxers for years. His very elderly boxer, Jess, had had a massive fit and, although he recovered, after a few days of deterioration we decided the kindest thing to do was to put him to sleep. As I'm sure many of you can imagine, the man was heartbroken. A few days later he popped in to have a chat about things and bring in a thank-you card (which was so touching about Jess that the nurse and I were in tears as soon as we read it!). He had his young and very beautiful other dog with him. I thought that we knew each other well enough for me to broach the subject and I asked him about the docking situation. He asked about the procedure and the reasons and gave it some consideration. After a few seconds he said he would be more than happy to have a Boxer with a tail because, spoken like what I would consider to be a true *lover* of the breed, he said, 'A boxer's a boxer to me whether it's got a tail or not. I'd definitely have one with a tail'. This heartened me greatly.

It is also extremely likely that breeders are still breaking the law by docking puppies themselves. There are numerous cases documented by the RSPCA such as the one where eleven Rottweiler puppies died as a result of docking. In fact, if I had the balls to put my money where my mouth is I would have asked every owner that comes in with a docked puppy who the breeder was. I would then either start bombarding the Royal College with names or I would contact the breeders and ask who had carried the docking

122

One of the eleven puppies that died
following tail docking.
© RSPCA

11 puppies that died following tail
docking.
© RSPCA

out. Until now this has all been too hard to prove but, as I said, times are indeed changing for the better.

The truth is that docking *is* painful. It takes away a dog's ability to communicate with other dogs. There is the risk of haemorrhage at the time and spinal infections and even death later on. There is some evidence of a link between docking and problems with the nerve supply to the bladder and rectum. There is also evidence of a link between docking and the development of perineal hernias. I have seen puppies that chew their stumps because of the discomfort. I have seen ones that knock the end of their stumps every time they sit down. There is *no* excuse any more.

In the Kennel Club book there are approximately fifty-two breeds in which docking is optional or, in most cases, 'customary'. It also specifies how much should be lopped off to meet the breed standard. I have heard of judges that have held their hand up when judging to block the offending appendage from view. Indeed the book does now tell you what the tail 'should' look like when it is present. In the case of the Old English sheepdog, which is customarily docked right to the base, the tail, when present, should be 'unobtrusive' and 'never curled or carried over back'. Is this so we can pretend it isn't there? I have had the pleasure of seeing two undocked examples of this breed and the tail is like a wonderful, hairy flag waving wildly in the breeze. No such thing should ever be made to be 'unobtrusive'.

My sister Alice used to live in Copenhagen and I have visited her many times there. You do not see any docked pet dogs and when I mentioned it to her Danish partner he seemed a little bewildered at why I had even noticed and then horrified that such a practice actually took place. Having said that, he was also bewildered by our amazement at the fact that Danish trains run on time to the minute. As he so rightly said, 'How can a train be delayed? There's nothing to get in their way.' Say no more.

As I said, we have recently made big advances with this issue with the passing of the new Animal Welfare Bill. I was closely involved with the tail-docking debate and continue to take a strong interest in what will happen next, as I know hundreds of vets do. There are a number of reasons for this interest.

In December 2005 I was getting very frustrated by the very small but very vocal minority of vets that were advocating the continuation of docking. I strongly believe that the majority of vets in the country are against the practice and wondered why no one seemed to be saying anything. I started a website so that vets would have an easy way to sign up and express their views. I wanted us, the profession with animal welfare at the core of our existence, to be heard by the politicians who were being bombarded by the pro-docking lobby. The veterinary profession does not particularly have a tradition of lobbying and many vets are so busy from day to day they simply don't have time to address these things or write letters or shout about it. However, because I am a lazy part-timer I did have the time!

I must admit that as the website went live I had a certain amount of trepidation because I suddenly thought, 'What if I'm wrong?' I needn't have worried because the profession absolutely excelled themselves. Within days there were dozens signing up daily and by the time the vote came round a few months later we had hundreds of names on the list. Besides the general practitioners many of the people who signed up are specialists in ethics, welfare, physiology and surgery. These people know what they are talking about. As I said before, I cannot speak for the rest of the profession in this book. If you would like to hear their opinions then go to www.vetsagainstdocking.co.uk. I know you will find it a fascinating read.

I mentioned before that I have spoken to many nurses who are against docking and they tend to be very vocal about the issue. However, since getting involved with the vets on this issue I have now heard from many vets who have themselves docked in previous years. Without fail they support the fact that it is painful and cruel. One vet started insisting that the breeders stayed in the room while it was done and soon found that many of them stopped having their puppies docked. I have heard similar stories from breeders. Many of my critics will say that I cannot comment on this issue because I have no first-hand knowledge of it. The first-hand evidence and *thousands* of years of combined experience of the Vets Against Docking will, I hope, speak for itself.

The fact is that I qualified in 1996 and I was not taught how to dock tails except therapeutically. I don't know when the universities stopped teaching it but it speaks volumes. I'm pretty sure that over time the practice will now just fizzle out simply because as younger vets come through there simply won't be anyone who will consider it ethical to perform it. The fact is that today the practice is carried out by a small number of vets who tend to be among the older members of the profession. They may well feel that we 'young whipper-snappers' don't know what we are talking about, but ultimately we, as professionals, should keep up to date with current thinking on all animal-related issues. We must also be guided by our governing body, the Royal College of Veterinary Surgeons, who released the following press statement at the time the Animal Welfare Bill was being considered:

The Council of the Royal College of Veterinary Surgeons (RCVS) has unanimously agreed to support an amendment to the Animal Welfare Bill prohibiting tail-docking in dogs, except for therapeutic purposes.

This would be subject to a review after five years, to take stock of scientific evidence of any change in the incidence of tail injuries in dogs during this period.

Currently, the *RCVS Guide to Professional Conduct for Veterinary Surgeons* accepts that docking may be permissible if it is for therapeutic or truly prophylactic reasons. This guidance will be reviewed if Parliament decides to change the law. The RCVS hopes that Parliament will make all non-therapeutic docking unlawful.

If the law is changed, a veterinary surgeon who docks a tail in circumstances not permitted by the amended law will be at risk of prosecution, as well as disciplinary action by RCVS.

'For some time the RCVS has been firmly opposed to the docking of dogs' tails without good clinical reasons,' comments Mrs Lynne Hill MRCVS, RCVS President. 'In 1993, when the law was changed and our current guidance laid down, it was hoped that cosmetic docking would in effect stop. Veterinary surgeons were advised then that they should only undertake therapeutic and "truly prophylactic" docking, and docking by anyone else was banned. Yet evidence suggests a lot of non-therapeutic docking is still being carried out, whether by veterinary surgeons or others.

'A ban with any exemptions is very difficult to enforce and this proved to be the case with tail-docking. It has proved hard to gather sufficient evidence to hear cases against veterinary surgeons who may have transgressed the guidance. We have come to the conclusion that it is time to stop prophylactic docking altogether.

'Animal welfare must be to the fore in any decision made by RCVS Council, and with a new Animal Welfare Bill going through Parliament this seemed like an excellent opportunity to call for a ban on all but therapeutic docking in dogs,' she concludes.

Many people feel a moratorium after a period of time would be the sensible option. How can we ever truly assess whether preventative docking is necessary unless we stop docking? The laughable thing is that it is widely believed that docking originated as a way for peasants to avoid a certain form of tax and had nothing to with injuries at all.

At the time of writing, the Scottish Executive plans to totally ban all non-therapeutic tail docking and it looks likely that Wales will vote a similar way. As for England, our MPs voted for a ban on all non-therapeutic docking except for truly working dogs that are customarily docked. It is this exemption that is still to be wrangled out and is the biggest cause for concern for vets. As the RCVS stated exemptions are very difficult to enforce. It will be vets that must certify these animals as likely to work, but as we have said time and again how can anyone know at five days of age whether an animal will work or not? Time will tell, as with all things.

During all the debates a lot of evidence was heard from the Continent and countries worldwide that have already banned docking in various forms. Several European countries made suggestions about where they feel they struggled to enforce the law and I believe this led to the single most important part of the proposed legislation; the banning of the showing of docked animals (in shows where the public have to pay for entry) except when demonstrating *working* ability.

The reason this is so crucial is the same reason that docking has continued unabated since the ban in 1993. Breeders believe that their dogs will not do well in shows if undocked. The show industry has driven this practice for decades and the outdated views of the higher echelons of the show world will now have to be closely examined. Previously, all puppies would be docked in case one ended up being shown. Now, for the show ring, the whole litter will be left with their tails. It is only a matter of time until people get used to what these dogs are supposed to look like; that is, with their tails as nature intended. I hope in twenty years' time children will look at old photos of docked dogs and wonder why on earth it went on in this day and age and be grateful that common sense prevailed.

Caffreys.
© Mr and Mrs Carmichael

127

The Bigger They Are...

The conventional end of this phrase goes, of course, '...the harder they fall.' But in the context of dog breeding and veterinary science, it might be amended to read, '...the younger they die' and applied to the inherent weakness we have bred into our dogs by making them giants.

Giant breeds are dogs such as the St Bernard, Newfoundland, mastiffs, Pyrenean mountain dog, Irish wolfhound, Leonberger and, of course, the epitome of the giants, the Great Dane. I have heard many people say of such dogs, 'They're too big for their hearts.' The truth is that these giant breeds and other larger breeds have an array of health problems (as, indeed, do most pedigree dogs). It's also true that small dogs on the whole live longer than large ones.

An article in the *Veterinary Record* in 1999 by A.R. Michell looked at the 'longevity of British breeds of dog and its relationships with sex, size, cardiovascular variables and disease'. Of the dogs in the study it found that the Bernese mountain dog, bullmastiff, flat-coated retriever, Great Dane, Irish wolfhound, Rhodesian ridgeback, Rottweiler and the St Bernard all had median ages at death of less than nine years. By contrast, Jack Russells, toy poodles, whippets, some terriers and, of course, the good old cross-breed had median ages of more than thirteen years, almost 50 per cent longer than their large counterparts. This would be like one family of humans dying on average thirty years earlier than others. You'd soon start to question why.

The fact is that with so many of these cases we have come to accept it as the norm. I know many people who would not be at all surprised if their giant dog died at the age of eight. Indeed, they are often very surprised and amazed if they last any longer. The fact is that we should be questioning this. I would have been horrified if Penny had died much earlier than she did, let alone *eight years* before she did. It is the same as people accepting that boxers faint and bulldogs snore. This is not normal and it should not be considered normal any more. If Pan collapsed while out walking I would be investigating every possible cause, not just saying, 'Yeah, he does that.'

When I worked in Tewkesbury I had the great pleasure to meet a young woman named Rachel and her first ever dog, Dudley. He was a gorgeous eight-week-old Great Dane. She absolutely adored him. Because he was a Dane we carefully went into all the reasons why she had to be careful with his nutrition and speed of growth. These breeds are predisposed to growth defects and joint problems because of the sheer extent of growing they have to do. They should be matured relatively slowly so that everything has time to develop properly.

He had a few puppy problems but nothing major. We had him in regularly because we were tracking his growth carefully. We all became very attached to him. Anyway, just after he turned one, Rachel went on a well-deserved holiday. Dudley was left in the hands of some very good friends with a large house and a large garden.

I was driving home for a rare lunch break one day when I had a call from the surgery asking me to go on an urgent visit to these people's house where they 'thought Dudley was dead'. This seemed incredible to me and I thought there must be some misunderstanding or crossed wires somewhere along the line. I drove straight to the house and there he was, flat out on one side in the garden, stone dead. It was a beautiful sunny day and the carers had been pottering about in the garden and Dudley was loping around intermittently chasing butterflies and sleeping in the shade of a big tree. One minute he had been fine and the next dead. I was devastated and I knew that Rachel would be absolutely distraught because she had devoted so much to him. He was such a sweet dog too; it just seemed unbelievable. He had died of a heart attack. For him it was probably a blessing. He was playing in the sun and then there was nothing. Many of these dogs develop heart disease and can endure a prolonged decline, usually requiring months, if not years of medication. At least he was spared that.

The truth is that I have seen two other Danes die of heart failure before the age of four, even though I don't see many Danes. I know we love these gentle giants, but isn't it time we let them shrink a little? I met a man in the village recently who is now on his third Dane. We got talking and he informed me proudly that all his had lasted until they were ten to twelve years old. This is sadly becoming more and more rare. He then went on to say that they always picked the runt of the litter. They always tried to get the one that was smallest. This worked well for him and his dogs. Having said that, I also know that one of Mark's clients who dotes on his Dane also got the runt and she has had a lifetime at the surgery for one thing or another.

According to Gough and Thomas the prevalence of the type of heart disease called dilated cardiomyopathy (DCM) has a prevalence of 3.9 per cent in the breed compared to 0.16 per cent in mixed breeds. This may not sound like a large number but when you consider this means that the disease is *twenty-four* times more prevalent in Danes than the average mongrel it suddenly comes into perspective. Heart disease is not just restricted to the Dane. For example the prevalence in Newfoundlands is eight times higher than in mixed breeds and in the St Bernard is sixteen times more prevalent. The Irish wolfhound is the worst with a prevalence of 5.6 per cent, thus being *thirty-five* times higher than in mixed breeds.

Besides heart disease there are also other conditions that are much more likely to be seen in giant breeds or the larger or heavier breeds such as Rottweilers, setters, Labradors, retrievers and hounds such as the bloodhound. The growth diseases we see such as hip dysplasia, elbow dysplasia and OCD are more commonly seen among these dogs. Many of these breeds are also unfortunately predisposed to bone tumours. Some of these tumours are incredibly aggressive, very painful and have very poor survival rates. Breeds affected are the Rottweiler, St Bernard, boxer, Great Dane and the Irish wolfhound.

I once had a client with a beautiful Rottie called Alice. She was an absolute diamond of a patient and had a great temperament. She had come in at the age of seven with lameness. She was a very big dog and we hoped she had just over done it. However, with the breed diagnostic tool we use so often she had a different list of differentials to a mongrel or, for that matter, most small dogs. She showed very little response to pain relief and a swelling appeared rapidly over the following few days. X-rays and further tests confirmed our worst fears that a tumour was present and Alice had to be euthanased within weeks because of the pain. It was a tragic case, as was the skull tumour I saw in 2005 in another very sweet Rottie called Petra. These animals and their owners went through horrible times that would not have happened before breeding went too far.

The Kennel Club undertook a survey recently in conjunction with the British Small Animal Veterinary Association (BSAVA) scientific committee. The survey was into the health of purebred dogs. The individual results for each breed can be found on the Kennel Club website and make interesting reading. According to this survey, cancer, and specifically bone tumours, accounted for 27 per cent of Newfoundland deaths, 33.9 per cent of Irish wolfhound deaths and a staggering 45.3 per cent of Rottweiler deaths.

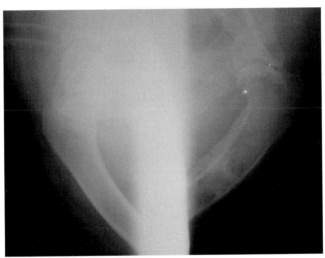

Giant breed osteosarcoma; X-ray of unaffected humerus on left of photo and cancerous humerus on the right.

© Emma Milne

Inherited Disease: 'One day, son, all this could be yours'

One of the things I absolutely love about my job is the clients. I know this may sound dubious in the light of some of the comments I made earlier in the book, but as I said, the bad ones are the minority. Clients are a constant surprise and it is what makes the job interesting. Because, in small-animal work, we often see people for very short, intense periods of time, it is difficult to get to know them unless you see them very frequently or work somewhere for a long time. Recently I had a client who came in with his Scottish deerhound. I'd seen him a few times previously for boosters for this dog and his good friend, their lurcher. This time he had a very swollen and painful eye and I had asked him to come back to see me to make sure the problem was totally sorted. The client is a doctor who works in accident and emergency and has always been lovely to deal with. (I suspect doctors and vets encounter a lot of the same frustrations!)

On the day of the check-up I was very pleased to see that the eye was fully returned to normal and his owner was just about to leave when he said, 'You know, I'm sure these things are getting overbred. Just look how deep his eyes are in the sockets.' I felt such relief when he said that and completely unprompted by me. It made me realise that many of my clients will totally understand what I am talking about in this book and that so many people already feel like this. Anyway, seeing an opening I said that I was glad he had said that and told him about my concerns with our pedigrees. He said (and this is what I mean when I say clients are a constant, refreshing surprise), 'I know, when we got him we were given this fifteen-generation pedigree and it's all the same f***ing names on it hundreds of times!' Well, I had to chuckle. It's rare that people are that open about something and I was pleased he felt he could be with me.

The point of the story is that he is not alone in this finding and the practice of mating closely related animals has caused a storm in the genetics of our dogs and accounts for many problems.

According to the *Collins English Dictionary*, the definition of the word 'pedigree' is: 1) the line of descent of a purebred animal 2) a document recording this 3) a genealogical table, especially one indicating pure ancestry 4) derivation or background. The definition then goes on to state that the history of the word comes from the Old French *pie de grue*, 'crane's foot', alluding to the spreading lines used in a genealogical chart. In simple terms, it just means a family tree.

Knowing this, I have pondered why the word conjures up the notion of a higher class of mutt. Why do we feel that pedigrees are more desirable than a cross-breed? I think there are several reasons. First, we pay a large amount of money for them. This appeals to our subconscious perception of worth. Surely an £800 Norfolk terrier is 'better' than a £75 mongrel dog from the local rescue centre in the same way that a £100,000 sports car is 'better' than a £10,000 hatchback. The analogy goes further, it's just occurred to me, because the sports car is probably much more likely to go wrong and the parts will cost you a bloody fortune! Second, I think it is because the word 'pedigree' is often used interchangeably with the word 'purebred'. The word 'pure' also conjures up images of untainted and unspoilt lineage. Third, I believe it is marketing over the years from companies such as Pedigree pet foods and Pedigree ales. We always associate the word with the best of the best but this is far from true when it comes to our dogs and cats. If a pedigree is a family tree then many these days are covered in mouldy fruit.

Most of what I have told you so far are problems that our dogs have because of the shape we have imposed on them. I have made the problems appear separate from inherited disease. I wanted to do this because I want you to start considering the deviations of shape from the starting point of the wolf and because I think looking at conformation makes these deformities easier to see and understand. However, by the very nature of the fact that it is the physical characteristics that have dictated the selection of these animals they must also be inherited. In this chapter I want to examine the other diseases and conditions that have been inadvertently and unwittingly selected for along with the outward appearance of the animals, such as the syringomyelia I spoke about earlier.

The sad fact is that there are now around *four hundred* inherited or predisposed conditions in our pedigree dog breeds. By predisposed I mean that we see a higher incidence of some conditions in certain breeds, even though the exact mode of inheritance has yet to be found. Nonetheless they are well documented and well recognised by vets. This would never happen in nature. These breeds would simply not survive without medical intervention or selective breeding. The list is, as you may well imagine, very long and very complex. It is a whole book on its own. What stuns me is that we have got to this point. The veterinary profession knows all about it, the Kennel Club knows all about it but the public are still being led to believe that by buying a pedigree dog they are buying the best dog they can get. Insurance companies charge more for pedigree dogs. Some clients believe this is because they cost more to buy or because they are more special than a scruffy, 'budget' mongrel. The fact is that it is more expensive to insure a pedigree dog because the companies' risk assessors know they will be very likely to pay out more for the average pedigree over its lifetime than for a mongrel.

At work I tend to see mongrels for cut pads, vaccinations, fight wounds, pulled muscles, road accidents and sickness brought on by raiding the bin. I see pedigrees for all these things, too, but the vast majority of the time I see them for reasons of their breed and their breed alone. This has got to stop.

I will try to give you an insight into some of these diseases and the worst examples. I think the thing that upsets me most about inherited disease is that it has come about as a *direct* result of breeding to the breed standard. By selecting for certain attributes that are visible on the exterior of the dog we have condensed the gene pool and ended up selecting for diseases too.

Although there are now many health schemes in place to eradicate these, as I said, they do not go far enough as yet. What is considered 'normal' for one breed of dog should be seen as what it is – we have created a number of breeds that are simply non-viable. This may sound dramatic but in many cases it's true. Without human-dictated selection pedigree dogs would not exist. We'll look at some of the breeds most affected either by number of problems or severity of particular conditions.

134

The German shepherd dog

This is a really popular breed but can be extremely unfortunate. At university we would often get asked about breed predispositions in exams. In hindsight this speaks volumes doesn't it? Breed specific disease is so 'normal' now that we get tested on it at university. If you were ever stuck in an exam, putting German shepherd dog down was usually a safe bet. According to Gough and Thomas, German shepherds have roughly 135 diseases or conditions to which they are predisposed or are inherited. The list takes seven and a half pages of the book! This is a staggering number and is way too much to go into here. Gough and Thomas is available from Blackwell Publishing! Some examples are conditions such as hip dysplasia, epilepsy, dwarfism, OCD- another growth defect, two types of clotting disorders, cataracts, cleft palates and heart defects to name but a few. They are also a breed that is not uncommonly seen with aggressive tumours of the spleen and or heart.

The Cavalier King Charles spaniel

Another increasingly sad case. I have to say that I think Cavaliers are probably the best-natured dogs you will ever come across. I have never in fifteen years of university and practice come across a single nasty one. This is pretty rare because there are usually one or two specimens of every breed that can be a bit grumbly or downright savage. In a way the diseases these dogs get are made even sadder by the fact they're such lovely, sweet dogs.

We mentioned earlier the condition affecting the base of the brain in these dogs called syringomyelia. By far the best-known disease the breed suffers from is a type of heart disease called endocardiosis or chronic degenerative mitral valve disease (CDMVD). The exact mode of inheritance is as yet unknown but we do know it is highly heritable. The disease is progressive and the affected valve undergoes changes over the life of the dog and a murmur develops. Heart valves should form a strong, blood-tight seal so that when the heart pumps blood it is pushed in one direction only. When valves in these dogs get diseased the seal is poor and blood can regurgitate in the wrong direction during the forceful beat. It is the noise of this regurgitation that can be heard as a murmur. Murmurs decrease the efficiency of the heart and increase the workload on it. As time goes by the extra load causes changes throughout the heart and can lead to heart failure and early death.

Cavaliers have a prevalence of the disease roughly twenty times higher than other dogs according to Gough and Thomas and an incredible 59 per cent of dogs over the age of *four* in this country have a murmur. Most Cavaliers have a murmur by the age of ten. The KC/BSAVA health survey showed that 42.8 per cent of Cavaliers died from heart disease.

We are fortunate to live in a time where we have excellent drugs

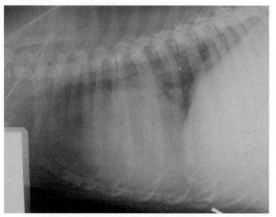 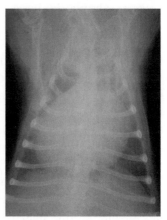

| Side view of the enlarged heart of a Cavalier King Charles spaniel. © Emma Milne | Midline view of the enlarged heart of a Cavalier King Charles spaniel © Emma Milne |

to help with most conditions. Most drugs available for heart disease do not reverse or cure the condition but do prolong life and alleviate the symptoms. These drugs can make a big difference in some cases but the fact that medicine and surgery has come such a long way should not make it acceptable to continue breeding dogs with this level of disease.

You can imagine my dismay when, as has often happened, I examine a six-year-old dog and say to the owner, 'Were you aware that she has heart disease?' and the owner says, 'Oh, yes, my last five of these died of heart failure. It is a problem, isn't it?' For God's sake! This is another prime example of an abnormality being considered normal and acceptable. In my head I hear a very exasperated sigh, the teeth clench and the urge to say 'Why don't you stop buying them then?' is painfully suppressed. The reason people don't stop buying them is that they are lovely dogs and many people have an affinity for a certain breed and because we *know* Cavaliers die of heart failure, Dobermanns die of heart failure, Rotties die of bone cancer, German shepherds die of ruptured splenic tumours and Labradors tolerate years of arthritic pain until their poor owner can't bear to see them like it anymore and has the poor thing put out of its misery. Yes, I know it is a massive generalisation and of course it's not true in all cases, but it is true in *too many* cases to be considered acceptable.

Besides heart disease, brachycephalic obstructive airway syndrome (see page 104) and the fact their brain doesn't fit in their head anymore, Cavaliers are also prone to nine different eye conditions, eight of which are known or suspected to be inherited. Surely those of you out there that are lovers of this breed would like to see this addressed?

Having said that, three of these conditions are screened for on the BVA/KC/ISDS eye scheme so reputable breeders can start to improve things. Cavalier breeders are well aware of the heart disease. The Cavalier King Charles Spaniel Club of the UK started a screening procedure in 1990 with the help of a cardiologist and a geneticist. The trouble with the heart disease is that many dogs do not develop a murmur until they are older and have already been bred from. Breeders or owners take their dog to any veterinary surgeon and they have their chest listened to. If there is no murmur present a form is signed to certify that and they are reassessed yearly. It was suggested that all dogs and bitches used for breeding should be at least two and a half years old and have clear hearts and should also have parents with clear hearts at or over the age of five years.

Unfortunately little progress has been made, possibly due to early, low-grade murmurs being missed or the fact that the scheme has not been taken up by all breeders (I have been asked to certify just *one* since I qualified). The club is now proposing a much more detailed scheme using cardiac specialists and ultrasound scans which are much more accurate and also tell a CDMVD murmur from other types. I hope with all *my* heart that the scheme gets the go-ahead and that somehow it can be made compulsory. I would love to start seeing these dogs racing around at fifteen or sixteen like Jack Russells often do!

West Highland white terriers

These dogs can have a lovely nature and are extremely popular. In the ten years I have been qualified I have seen very few Westies that did not have skin disease. These dogs commonly suffer with a number of skin complaints such as yeast infections, seborrhoea, food hypersensitivity and most commonly atopy. Atopy is usually characterised by multiple allergies and causes intense itching which can be worse in the summer due to allergens like pollen, grass and fleas. Some benefit from hyposensitisation but investigation and treatment can become extremely expensive and many dogs require lifelong medication just to keep the disease under control. The affected dogs are miserable and scratch constantly.

I'm getting pretty tired of seeing these as puppies and asking if the owners have ever had one before. They usually say no and then I have to explain all the things they need to look out for. You see, besides the skin problems they are prone to a number of other problems. One is called 'craniomandibular osteopathy'. This is where, as they grow, they develop an extremely painful bony swelling on the jaw. It can usually be controlled with pain-relief and is self-limiting, meaning they simply grow out of it. However, some severe cases do not respond to treatment and the dogs require surgery to remove part of the mandible. They are also prone to another condition found in humans called Legg-Perthe's disease. This is another developmental disease in which the top of the femur (where the ball of the hip joint is) loses its blood supply and dies. The only option is surgery to remove the dead piece of bone. This is highly invasive and can have a very long recovery time.

In fact I had a patient called Robbie whom I treated in Cheltenham. His owner rang the surgery late one Friday and left a message for me and my boss to say she was thinking of buying a Westie and what did we think? The message got relayed to us on Monday and I clearly remember as Emma the nurse came through to ask us, Julie, the other nurse, and I all chorused in unison, 'Don't!' We did have a little laugh at the time at the outburst and one of us went off to phone the lady and explain our reservations. The lady had in fact not been able to contain herself and had already bought the wee thing over the weekend. Robbie soon came for a check-over and he was what every Westie is – irresistibly cute as a puppy. He was a great little dog and everyone at the surgery fell in love with him.

Unfortunately he had intestinal problems from the word go. He then developed Legg-Perthe's disease and had his hip removed and by the time I left to move north he was showing early signs of atopy. He didn't deserve any of it and nor did his owner. All through all his treatments he soldiered on and never once complained or growled or resisted. Obviously this is a bad case but it is a fact nonetheless.

Boxers

I actually see lots of boxers where I work now and on the whole they are very good dogs to deal with at work. I can't think of any off the top of my head that are aggressive and generally the breed are pretty well known for their nice nature. The only thing that usually gives me a slight sense of apprehension when I see one on the list is the fact that most boxers have something in common with A.A. Milne's gorgeous character Tigger and that is their bounce! It is incredibly difficult to inject 30 kilos of muscle, sinew and, often, slobber when it is pinging round the room like a lunatic! I have some boxer patients that are respectable old men and women now and they have a very reserved air about them and are lovely to have in.

Boxers are another breed that have had the misfortune to have developed faulty hearts as their features have changed. They are predisposed to six heart conditions, one of which is actually named after them. They can develop the dilated cardiomyopathy that we mentioned earlier and have a prevalence twenty-one times higher than a mixed breed. They are also known to faint. They can be affected by many different types of skin disease including atopy and acne, but perhaps their biggest concern beside their hearts is their predisposition to cancer. For some reason boxers are quite commonly seen with various types of tumours, and sitting here now I can think of four immediately that I have operated on in the last year. Some types are more common than others but I am always more wary of lumps and bumps in this breed than some others.

Cocker spaniels

This very popular spaniel is one where the difference between the show variety and the working variety is practically a chasm. Field cockers tend to have much less exaggerated features such as the ears and are generally more robust. Cockers' skin is prone to many conditions, including the typical spaniel ears, and they can have a number of other problems, but it's their eyes that are possibly their biggest area for concern. According to Gough and Thomas, between the American and English types, they are prone to twenty-five different eye conditions, some of which can be screened for. Springer spaniels are also prone to a high number of eye conditions.

Dobermanns
Although Dobermanns have a fierce reputation they are generally very sweet dogs in my experience. My previous boss, Alison, had a gorgeous old lady of a Dobermann called Portia. She would gamely try and play with the boys when we took her with us, but they would steadfastly ignore her and she would gambol about near them just to feel part of the gang. Portia developed heart disease as she got older and none of us were surprised. Dilated cardiomyopathy is practically a given in this breed and Dobermanns account for *half* of the cases that are seen. Portia also went on to develop disc disease in her neck and had to go to Bristol University for decompression surgery. Nothing fazed her and she managed on

Ali and Portia.
© Alison Jones

140

heart medication and thyroid medication (another condition Dobermanns are predisposed to is hypothyroidism) for some years before sadly having to be put to sleep. She's greatly missed.

Another condition quite commonly seen in Dobermanns is 'wobbler' syndrome. This sounds humorous but is a malformation of the bones in the neck. The spinal cord gets compressed and the dogs stop being able to walk in a coordinated way and the majority will require spinal surgery. The breed is also the most commonly seen with Von Willebrand's disease in which they fail to clot blood sufficiently. This can be a major risk factor at the time of any surgery or accident.

Labradors (lovely Samba with OCD both elbows, Jazz with a hip score of 96 and Elgar with Cushings), schnauzers, golden retrievers, dachshunds, Pekinese, bassets, poodles and so on and so on. These dogs have multiple breed problems that can affect them. There simply is too much to go into here. All this is on top of all the defects, deformities and disease conditions we looked at in the previous chapters.

The fact is that this is just a drop in the ocean of problems our pedigrees are suffering from. Only today I was flicking through the BSAVA *Manual of Small Animal Neurology* and came across a list of breed-related neurological disorders. There are 151 recorded in dogs and cats. Many are affected by more than one and our friend the German shepherd is predisposed to *nine*. If you really want to get a particular breed I implore you to research it thoroughly. Talk to your vet *before* you get the dog. Most vets would be more than happy to give pre-purchase advice. That way you can learn what health schemes the parents should have been involved in, what diseases or conditions you are likely to encounter and how much time you and your dog are likely to spend at the vets. You wouldn't buy a house without a survey, so don't do the same with a dog.

The British Bulldog: Symbol of an Empire

Profile of an English bulldog.
© Emma Milne

This dog (officially called the English bulldog) is described by the Kennel Club as a 'delightfully ugly dog'. It also says that after 1835 it 'began to evolve into the shorter-faced, more squat version we now know'. Surely these dogs did not naturally 'evolve' this way. We *bred* them to be this way. An ironic fact is that this poor dog is held as the symbol of our 'empire'. At one time it was a strong and athletic breed bred for bull-baiting. It was selected to have a slightly longer lower jaw to allow it to breathe while it hung onto the bull. These days it is almost unrecognisable in that respect and would hardly be able to keep pace with a bull let alone breathe through its nose while stressed. Saying that the modern-day bulldog is a symbol of the 'best of British' is like saying that football hooligans are something to be proud of.

With the skin-fold infections, deformed and protruding jaws and brachycephalic obstructive airway syndrome that we have discussed

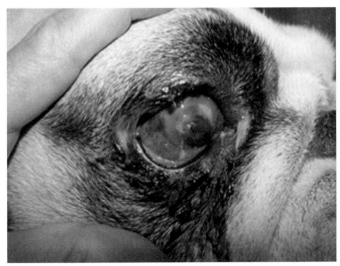

A bulldog with a ruptured eye after ulceration.

earlier come the inherited and predisposed traits: distichiasis (misplaced eye lashes that can sometimes cause ulceration), cleft palates, aortic and pulmonic stenosis (abnormalities of the major blood vessels at the heart) and cherry eye (discussed below). Bulldogs are also one of the smaller breeds to suffer with hip dysplasia. Not many have been hip scored – in fact only 16 as of January 2006 – but the breed mean score is 41. These dogs were presumably put forward for screening because of their breeding potential in other respects.

A friend of mine who is a vet had a client with a bulldog that developed cherry eye. This is fairly common in this breed and many of the brachycephalic types. There is a gland in the third eyelid that contributes to the production of tears and this gland prolapses out. The majority of them require surgery to replace the gland and there are various techniques. In cases that recur the gland is sometimes removed. However, we always leave this as a last resort because once removed the dog will be much more likely to get 'dry eye' later in life, another painful and chronic condition to which the breed is predisposed.

This particular dog was booked in to have the operation and on arrival the owner told the vet that a bulldog breeder had told him to request the removal of the gland because so many recur and it was bound to need taking out anyway. A long discussion ensued

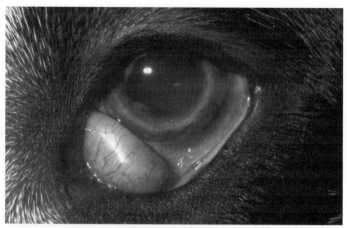

Cherry eye – the prolapsed gland in the third eyelid.
© Dr David Gould

during which the vet tried to talk sense but the owner was adamant that the gland be removed. The fact is that surgical techniques evolve all the time and many of these operations are curative now. Vets are often up against a certain type of breeder that believes they know more about a particular breed than their vet. This is very rarely the case and in this case the all-knowing breeder had severely compromised the future of this dog's tear production.

This attitude among breeders and owners is hardly surprising when the following is found on the bulldog rescue website when advising owners about when their bulldog may require surgery. On the subject of cherry eye:

'This does need surgery but don't allow the vet to stitch it back in, it almost always comes back out when the stitches have dissolved. Insist it is snipped out, this breed is already predisposed to dry eye so it is not a valid argument for not snipping it, many bulldogs get dry eye later in life regardless due to blocked tear ducts.' (This is also totally factually incorrect.)

This follows the information that the page 'should be taken purely as a guide and would be the standard advice given, obviously we are not vets but these are the most common surgery areas where we disagree with the majority of vets.' I'm sure you can understand why our blood pressure rises when we hear this kind of thing.

144

Does anyone perhaps think that if they are disagreeing with *the majority of vets* that maybe they might just be wrong? Take advice on your animal's health from your veterinary surgeon. They have a veterinary degree. Please don't compromise the welfare of your animal because of what an untrained lay person tells you.

The dog in question is severely undershot and has distichiasis, but the owner was determined that he wanted to breed from her. Within a few months of her eye operation the dog developed a uterine infection called a pyometra. These can be treated medically with antibiotics and drugs to stimulate the cervix to open to allow the pus to come out. However, the infection can be very serious and can actually be fatal in some cases. Also, those that are treated medically tend to recur with each passing season. It was strongly recommended that she be spayed, which is the treatment of choice in most cases, but no, she must be used for breeding. The dog was hospitalised for fluids and the necessary medication and the pyometra cleared up. Sure enough it recurred and after more treatment was eventually spayed. At this point she was less than eighteen months old.

Perhaps the most unethical and disgusting thing that has happened to the breed is that many of them can no longer give birth naturally. Thus, you have the situation whereby many bulldogs are given caesareans. Not only is this totally unnecessary surgery (were it not for the breed standard) but they are also one of the breeds that is most at risk from an anaesthetic! Their deformed airways and excess tissue in the mouth make them much more at risk of post-operative complications because once the tube in their windpipe is removed their airways are effectively non-existent. This *cannot* be right by any stretch of the imagination. McGreevy and Nicholas very rightly point out that 'The minimum performance requirement is to survive birth without assistance. Where genes can be passed from one generation to the next only with the intervention of a veterinarian who performs a caesarean section to overcome relative foetal oversize, it can be argued that both dam and offspring have failed an essential performance test.'

I was involved with a BBC programme called *Real Story* and they were doing a piece on bulldogs and I was interviewed because I have voiced concerns previously about these problems. After the programme a number of things happened. The Royal College received enough complaints about me to warrant a full disciplinary

145

hearing. The owners and breeders were very upset that I had slandered their breed so much and that I had given the impression that I was speaking on behalf of the profession. Again, I say I am not; these are my opinions. I can't get across enough that I don't hate bulldogs or any of the other dogs I've highlighted. I see each individual dog as a personality inside a body and these bodies vary, not the personality inside it. There are very few of these that I even dislike, let alone hate. Dogs are my favourite animals. I know people were upset because they love bulldogs. The bulldogs I have met and treated have been undeniably lovely dogs. I just wish I hadn't had to see the conditions I have done. I'm asking for some common sense from those who love the breed. I'm trying to highlight what I believe are major causes for concern as far as welfare is concerned and I am in no way in a minority.

Another thing that happened was that I went on breakfast television the next day to talk about the programme and the issues. There was a man there with a bulldog puppy and a champion breeder on a video link (presumably for my safety). I said that a lot of the birth difficulties were because of the narrow pelvis of the bitch and the very large heads of the puppies. This is generally held as one of the major reasons. The breeder launched into a tirade saying that I didn't even know what I was talking about because it was nothing to do with size differences and it was because a lot of bulldogs suffer from uterine inertia, meaning the uterus doesn't contract and they can't expel the pups. Uterine inertia may well be the cause of some difficulties but what she failed to realise is that she backed up everything I said. She didn't say they didn't have birthing difficulties; she totally agreed that they did. The opinion on why is pretty irrelevant. Without surgical intervention the breed would literally die out within a few generations.

The owner of the puppy that was in the studio and I went outside at one point for a cigarette break (I don't smoke anymore I'm glad to say) and we got chatting. He raised a point that he obviously believed to be true and which I've heard so many times before. He said that many bulldog breeders felt that vets rushed into doing caesareans on these animals and didn't give them long enough to see if they could give birth. He also said that some believed it was because it is such a lucrative thing for the vet. This really makes me very angry. From my viewpoint, the breed has an approximate 50 per cent incidence of dystocia, or difficulties giving

146

birth. The breed has a greatly increased risk of anaesthetic problems. The animals in question are not only of emotional importance to their owners, they are often extremely financially valuable and carrying a small fortune of puppies. If things go wrong we are buggered. Today's society is very quick to sue and how these births are managed could mean the difference between career or no career. Veterinary surgeries during the day have full staffing levels for not only monitoring anaesthesia but for resuscitation of the puppies and post-operative monitoring, and the best backup you can get in case of problems. Imagine the furore there would be if the vet waited to see if surgery could be avoided, by which time the placentas are separating, the bitch is getting more exhausted and the puppies are slowly being starved of oxygen. You finally decide you have to go ahead, by which time there is one vet and one nurse at the surgery and most of the pups die, and while the nurse is trying to revive a puppy or get some extra swabs or towels the mother has an anaesthetic crisis and the breeder loses ten grand's worth of prime bulldog in one fell swoop. We're damned if we do and we're damned if we don't.

We shouldn't be questioning whether it is right for the breed to become extinct; we should be pondering how long it will be until we simply can't save them any more.

With too many of these breeds we have come to accept abnormalities as normalities. This is fundamentally wrong and should not be accepted any more. If the breed standards need to be changed to such a degree that the dogs go back to looking like they did a century ago and they are all a little more similar to each other then so be it. It is the only way we can hope to alleviate the suffering.

The historical figure Edwina had told me about earlier was William Hogarth, the painter. His famous self portrait features (obviously) himself but also his beloved pug. He was well known for being a lover of the breed. I know that many of my opinions about changing the way our breeds look will be scoffed at by some of today's breeders who cannot tolerate the thought of the appearance changing. However, when you look at pictures such as the one I describe here, you can see how drastically we already *have* changed their appearance. The pug featured in this painting has longer, straight legs but virtually no skin folds at all and a very distinct muzzle, not one that is non-existent like today's pugs. I'm sure if

147

William Hogarth was to set eyes on the modern version of his beloved pet he would be, conversely, as horrified as those of you who wish to keep ours unchanged.

Self portrait of William Hogarth and his pug, 1745.
© Tate Britain

148

Mutts and Mongrels

I feel that as I have been so vocal regarding pedigrees I should say a few words about mongrels, or mutts as they are also known. I am obviously a big advocate of mongrels and I have thought long and hard about why they might have such a bad reputation.

I think part of it is because of the reputation of 'the rescue dog'. I think rescue dogs are often regarded as 'trouble children'. I read a book recently that I was sent by a book company in the hope that if I liked it I would recommend it to people. I won't even name it because I don't want to give it any publicity. At one point it actually said that all rescue dogs have behavioural problems. I was livid. It is exactly this attitude that means so many don't get homes. The problem is that many of these 'rescue' dogs are victims of circumstance or poor decision-making on the part of their owners. Agreed, some dogs can have problems because of poor socialisation, but the vast majority of these dogs can be turned around in a very short space of time. Let's not forget that there are also hundreds of pedigree dogs in rescue centres and breed rescue too.

There are thousands of completely 'normal' dogs at these places that have ended up being given up because of relationships breaking down or after the death of their owner. There is *nothing* wrong with them. Penny, my first dog, was destined for a shelter just because she wasn't house-trained. When we took her home she was house-trained within a week. That woman and her child missed out on sixteen years of companionship with a very gentle, sweet little dog. She was a mutt and extremely healthy.

I am a patron for a charity called Dogs Trust and have seen first hand what 'rescue' dogs are like. Pan and Badger were from an unwanted litter too but they have, touch wood, been superbly healthy. I love collie-crosses but would I have a purebred one? No. They are often neurotic and highly strung. They have an

149

enormous need for exercise and stimulation and most pet situations fall a long way short of providing this.

I think the main reason mongrels aren't sought after as much as pedigrees is that they are somehow looked down upon and seen as inferior. It is the opposite of what we said about why people want pedigrees. They seem to be worth more, so they must be better somehow. It's a prejudice apparent everywhere. Marketing often uses pedigree dogs for certain brands, while the typical 'scruffy' mongrel is used to denote a cheeky ruffian covered in mud or digging holes in the lawn. Even the classic Disney *Lady and the Tramp* says it too. The 'lady' is a posh spaniel and the 'tramp' a scruffy mutt.

There is also the fact that lots of people love certain types of dog and they want to know what they are getting. Temperament is obviously very important and people may worry that they won't know what the temperament of a mongrel is likely to be. There are a couple of points to raise here. One is that I see many breeds of dog at work that I wouldn't entirely trust. Speak to any vet and they will probably list the same dogs that they would be wary of when approaching for an examination. Mine would immediately be Jack Russells, Rottweilers, Great Danes, mastiffs, German shepherds, Shar Peis, corgis and Border collies, but the truth is I know some Labradors that are totally savage and it is well known that some springers, cockers and retrievers have a very nasty streak. The majority of 'well-educated' dogs have lovely natures, and most mutts and mongrels will be the same. Thinking about it, I rarely feel apprehension about a mongrel's temperament at work, unless it's obviously a cross of one of the above!

It is inevitable that some of you may have owned mongrels at one time that had the misfortune to be ill or have chronic problems. Of course, you can get genetic backfires in any dog, including mongrels. My point is that proper mongrels are healthier in general. I would implore all of you before you get a dog to consider a mongrel. Go to the shelters and have a look. Put your name down for a puppy if you feel a puppy would be more appropriate for you; you may have to wait but there are always unwanted litters being born, unfortunately.

The thing that always strikes me about mongrels and, as I have thought about this more and more, the thing that I love most about them is their uniqueness. Even in a litter of first crosses between

150

two pedigrees you will get a wonderful mixture of individuals. The true unrecognisable cross breeds are even better in my eyes. I love not knowing what they are and I love how individual they all are. When you want a dog just decide whether you want a big or a small or a fluffy or a smooth and give a mutt a try. I'm sure you won't regret it.

PART FOUR

THE TRUTH ABOUT CATS

The Good, the Bad and the Ugly

My cat, Brian, as a mischievous kitten.
© Emma Milne

When I embarked on this book my head was full of the aberrations that we have inflicted on dogs. Cats were really at the back of my mind because on the whole they have very few problems related to conformation because we haven't sought to alter their shape excessively. As I progressed further into the book, however, I began thinking about why I always consider cats to be so healthy when I think about them as a species. The fact is that the vast majority of cats I see are 'moggies', the cat equivalent of a mongrel.

The sheer number of moggies far outweighs the number of pedigrees, so this is what people are used to seeing. Many people get cats because they are considered low-maintenance pets and the thought of spending hours a day brushing a Persian, for instance, doesn't appeal. I also think that often people end up with cats when they least expected it. This may sound silly but in my work I have seen numerous cats that have arrived at someone's house and 'adopted' them. It is one of the characteristics of cats that many of us love – their independence. There are also many occasions where someone hears of someone that has a litter and then your kid badgers you into seeing them and, well, who can resist a kitten? Ultimately, I think most people see cats as cats and are not too concerned about their lineage.

As I said, cats have somehow escaped most shape-induced abnormalities of the kind we see in dogs. I think that the main reason for this is that historically cats have not been used for a variety of different jobs like dogs have, so they haven't needed to be subtly altered. Mostly they have been pets and hunters of rodents and other pests and their shape is already well-adapted for that.

However, as with dogs, as time has gone by and the show world has taken over, we have started exaggerating cats' features and inevitably have started to select for disease conditions along the way by concentrating solely on the physical appearance of the animal. As with dogs, we can take the alterations in body shape to examine where things have started to go wrong.

The most obvious breed for imposition of unnatural looks is the Persian. Now I have got into trouble before for an episode of *Vets in Practice* where I implied that many Persians were bad-tempered. I apologise, but many of the breed I have seen at work have been on the grumpy side of the spectrum. It was an observation. Perhaps my impression is heightened by the fact that they *look* so miserable. The fact is that if I had the life that many Persians endure I would be miserable too.

The shape of the face and skull is probably the feature we have most changed in our cat breeds. There are several breeds that have tended towards the flatter faces but by far the most extreme example of this is the Persian. These cats are also termed brachycephalic, the same as the short-faced dog breeds we have already discussed.

As time has gone by the flatness of the face in this breed has become more and more extreme; indeed, some of these cats seem to have *concave* faces now. I recently read a letter in a cat magazine from a Persian breeder of some twenty-odd years. She was extremely concerned about this trend towards the extreme type of face and was imploring breeders to be more sensible when it comes to selecting features. She was very sensible and was urging the breed as a whole to return to the more 'normal' face shape seen in the earlier examples of the breed. I hope they listen to her because this brachycephalic shape has led to a number of problems and, I

156

believe, a deterioration in their welfare. When we discuss these I will talk mostly about the Persian because it is the most extreme case, but the same models can be applied to a lesser degree to any cat breed with a flatter-than-normal face.

Today's Persians have very bulbous eyes, which are more prone to injury, ulceration and disease. As with the pug and the Pekinese I have seen more than one that have had one eye removed due to chronic disease or injury.

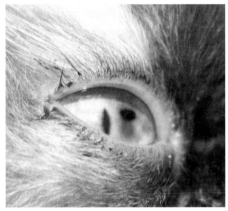

Chronic damage to the eye of a Persian cat.
© Emma Milne

Many Persians also have 'watery' eyes. I once had to present a prize to a winner of a competition. It was very local and I popped round one afternoon to have some photos taken. The winner was a very sweet, elderly couple and as I arrived they proudly showed me their three, prize-winning Persians. I was quickly informed that they had all come from the south and all from the same breeder over the years and that their dad had been Grand Champion. I was then told that the one trying to groom itself by the door 'always had trouble with knots' and that 'they all have those runny eyes'. I wasn't sure if they were referring just to their cats but I suspect that they meant the breed because most of the ones I've seen have this eye problem.

In fact Persians have what we call epiphora, which is an abnormal overflow of tears. Tears are constantly produced by normal animals and drain away down a small duct from the eye to the nose. When we produce an excess of tears such as when we cry the duct cannot drain them all and they overflow. We also very quickly get a runny nose because of the increase in tear fluid draining into the nose. In Persians the duct that should drain the tears tends to be very narrow and so cannot cope with a normal production of tears. Overflow occurs, often leading to 'undesirable' tear staining of the fur on the face. Indeed I have been asked on several occasions by owners of short-faced cats whether there is any kind of bleaching agent or wash that will get rid of the stain. The fact is if the animals hadn't been bred to have abnormal anatomy they would have no staining.

According to the Cat Fanciers' Association (CFA), the world's largest registry of pedigreed cats, 'the large eyes do mean that a certain amount of tearing is normal, and a daily face wash is recommended.' Note the interesting use of the word 'normal'. If any of my three cats had eyes that constantly watered I would be investigating the cause and seeking treatment.

Brachycephalic syndrome also means they may have 'stenotic nares', as we also saw in dogs, and these can in some cases lead to respiratory distress. Cats very much avoid mouth breathing whenever they can. We usually see panting if the cat is, for example, stressed at coming to the vets, but in Persians in particular the abnormal anatomy can be more serious and restrict airflow.

To a lesser degree than with the dogs we also see some deformation of tooth structure and position because the teeth have had to become rotated in order to fit in the shortened jaw. There are a couple of other examples of shape-changing. British Shorthairs, for example, have a shortened face, although not to the degree that the Persian has. It too may get runny eyes and skin-fold infections.

Going to the other extreme of face shape is the Siamese. My partner, Mark, is an absolute Siamese fan. He always had them when he was a child and he raves about their character and personality and I know many Siamese owners who do likewise. I also think they were *once* beautiful cats. However, over the years the pointed, fine features and slender build of the breed have been taken to the nth degree. The face is now extremely long and the cats appear gaunt. Their ears are now huge compared to their faces and they have started to resemble Gremlins. We also encounter many Siamese cats that suffer unduly with teeth and gum problems. Commonly, the canine teeth have become so long that they impinge on the opposite lips and can cause ulceration.

Although this long face has not caused such direct problems as

158

the short face of the Persian, the inbreeding that has contributed to it has weakened the breed genetically. We'll discuss that more in the next chapter.

A good friend of ours, Jenny, also a Siamese lover, has designed and made a fantastic type of cat bed that doubles as a carrier. In her attempts to get the product off the ground she has visited quite a few cat shows. Being interested in the breed she went to see them and was stunned at how they have changed. She herself now owns a Siamese cross that still looks like the cats that she and Mark fell in love with all those years ago.

Cat breeds have also had their beautiful coats tinkered with over the years. There are now all manner of colours and lengths of coat and types of fur but the two ends of the spectrum are the Persian, the Rex and the Sphinx.

The Persian is a good example of the unnaturally long-hair coat I mentioned when I discussed dogs. I'm sure the origin of the breed did not have fur like the modern ones do, but we have deemed that, over time, they should be as mop-like as possible. The consequence of this is that there are few vets in the country who will not have had to sedate or fully anaesthetise many a Persian at one time or another to fully shave the poor beast because it is a mass of knots. When I say a mass of knots, I mean it. I have done 'dematts' on these cats where they have been left with fur on their heads and their tails and that's all! It's like shearing a sheep. The fur is so matted that it comes away in one large sheet like a doormat.

I'm sure that I'll now get hundreds of letters saying that if you groom them from a young age and *bath* them as often as the CFA wants you to then this should never happen. Well, it does. That is a fact. I'm sure many people will be quick to judge and say it is the fault of the owners but I don't think this is fair. Many of these cats will not tolerate grooming, particularly round their nether regions and stomachs. I'm sure the sheer amount of time needed to tackle the grooming is probably quite a push for many working people and parents.

The fact is that this length of coat is totally unreasonable, unnatural and very often unmanageable. Indeed, the CFA informs us that, 'Their long, flowing coats require an indoor, protected environment.' I see, so we keep them all indoors and bath them once a week and groom them every day and wash their faces, and *then* we take them to the vet with their stress-induced cystitis and oxalate bladder stones they are especially prone to when kept solely indoors.

When we have these cats in now for dematting we always offer to clip all their fur short with clipper guards the same as you would do with a dog. We remove the mats to the skin but then effectively give them a short coat all over. Lots of people find it a great help in getting the grooming started again and the cats certainly seem happier.

Persian cats and other fine-long-haired cats can be carriers of ringworm and can be an important factor in the spread of disease to other cats. This occurs in households and catteries alike.

At the opposite end of the 'fur spectrum' is the sphynx cat. This is a rare breed at the moment but seems to be gaining popularity as many 'freaky' novelties do as time goes by. The sphynx is totally hairless. The Governing Council of the Cat Fancy (GCCF) – the cat equivalent of the Kennel Club – does recognise the breed but also gives a warning about its care: 'As these cats are virtually hairless they require particular care. Firstly, they have to have the sebaceous oils washed from their skin regularly because there is no hair to dissipate the oils and allow them to be removed naturally. Secondly, fur on cats helps to protect them from injury and cats without fur may suffer severely from scratches and playful bites which would not affect cats which have a coat. Thirdly, they need to be protected from cold and from strong sunlight because of the risk of sunburn and skin cancer.' The GCCF also says that it has no intention to register any other hair deficient breeds. How much more hair deficient can you get?

Their third point, I believe, is the cause for most concern. These cats are at quite a disadvantage when it comes to regulating their body temperature, as are hairless dog breeds. We see skin cancer quite commonly in cats with even white fur on their ear tips let alone a complete lack of it. Applying sun block to a whole cat is extremely likely to cause stress to the animal, be ineffective and result in a prolonged grooming session and removal of the cream. Even without development of skin cancer it is likely that these cats would get sun burn incredibly quickly if exposed. Coping with any level of cold is likely to be just as difficult.

Totally hairless cats would never survive in nature because of sun damage, chills and excessive fight wounds. We come back to

160

the ethical dilemma of whether we should be creating animals that are likely not to survive without human intervention.

Cats on the whole have not really encountered the extremes of shape alteration that we see in dogs but a couple of years ago I was alerted by a client to the phenomenon of 'Twisty Kats'. I had never heard of them but I looked on the internet and was left absolutely dumbfounded at the possibility that a human being has created this abomination. These cats have been deliberately bred to have shortened and totally bent front legs. You won't fully appreciate the horror of this until you see it so if you have internet access have a look. The 'creator' (a woman from Texas) proudly reports the cats make ideal house cats because they are so deformed that they are unable to scratch your furniture. Has the world gone completely mad? How can we live in a time when this is deemed acceptable or even legal? You are also warned that if you take one on you need to be careful about letting them go up and down stairs because they are so unbalanced that on the way down they often fall. Neither can they climb as cats love to do. I think this is possibly the most atrocious thing I have ever seen.

The woman who bred them now says that she only bred one litter from the dam and all the cats are neutered. She also points out on her website that she is doing nothing different from any other breeders. For instance, she goes on to mention (you've guessed it) the British bulldog. The reports about these cats caused a massive, global uproar from animals groups and everyday people who thought that it was disgusting. The cats have been called the 'cat equivalent of thalidomide victims'. The trouble is that the breeder does have a point but she has rapidly and shockingly produced a deformed cat that can not live the life that most of us would expect a cat to have.

Although this is obviously an extreme situation I heard an interview with Paris Hilton recently that left me equally angry. She was describing how she is an enormous lover of animals (let's not talk about the captive monkeys) and during the list of her pets she disclosed that she had two (I think) 'Munchkin kittens'. Steve Wright, who was interviewing her asked what they were and she said they were cats that had all four legs very short, 'about two inches long', and they are 'like so cute.' I drove home and got straight on the computer and was again amazed. These cats are everywhere. They have short legs and run like a ferret according to most of the websites I visited. There are many pictures and articles extolling their virtues and those of the woman who started the breed. The Munchkin enthusiasts are quick to point out that the defect happens naturally and at least two cats have been reported like it in history. I don't know the exact number of normal cats there are in the world but I would guess it is in the high millions, if not billions, so I'm guessing that two or three out of that number doesn't really make it that 'normal'. It is only right to point out here that the GCCF has 'no intention to recognise Munchkins or any similar breed'.

The adult cats of the breed are also called kittens because the breed keeps its kitten nature. Fantastic, kittens are way more fun than adults, aren't they, and for all those immature and irresponsible enough to want to inflict a genetic deformity on an animal for their own amusement I suppose they are ideal. No one seems to have pondered whether this long-term kittenishness coupled with the dwarfism desired in the breed is like a condition called pituitary dwarfism in dogs. In fact, I couldn't find any research into this lack of maturity at all. Astoundingly the only genetics I was bombarded with is the fact that every single Munchkin kitten in the whole of North America and maybe the world for all I know is descended from just *two* cats and their offspring. If this isn't the absolute epitome of inbreeding I don't know what is.

I'm a little surprised in this age of political correctness that no one seems to think it even slightly inappropriate to have named a whole breed after the vertically challenged characters from the *Wizard of Oz* played by actors with dwarfism. Maybe next year someone can mess around with some more animals and we could have a John Merrick puppy or an Alison Lapper kitten. Yes, it is madness.

In truth, it only seems mad to me because cats have escaped this madness for so long. Is it human nature to experiment and play God, and if so is it acceptable? I don't know why I'm so surprised about Paris's little cuties; we've been doing the same thing to dogs for centuries. I suppose it was only a matter of time before someone made a feline version of the dachshund.

Inherited Disease: The Accumulator Bet That Never Pays

As I said before, it can appear to the average vet and cat owner that cats are a very healthy species, but while doing the research into this book I have made some startling discoveries. Just the same as with dogs, as we have selected for the aesthetic qualities we desire in our cats we have gradually and inexorably bred in disease. As the gene pools have been reduced so these traits and defects have become more and more prevalent and in some cases have exceeded those of their canine companions. To date there are approximately 250 inherited diseases in cats, with more being identified all the time.

For what is probably the worst case we must return to our old friend the Persian. In Persians and some exotic shorthairs there is a condition called PKD, or polycystic kidney disease. This is a condition that the animals are born with and is inherited. The gist of the disease is that as the animals grow their kidneys start to develop large, fluid-filled cysts. These cysts generally progress until there is little or no normal kidney tissue left and the cats go into full-blown renal failure. Animals are born with the cysts but the size and number all vary a lot between cats.

There is no cure. Luckily nowadays we have medication and prescription diets that can help support the kidneys when they start to fail, but the bottom line is that this disease is a killer and all we can do with medicine is alleviate the symptoms and reduce the suffering. So, how much of a problem is it? You will probably be surprised to hear that the number of cats affected is *40 to 50* per cent. There have been various studies done in various countries and they have consistently agreed with this level. This means that roughly one out of every two Persians has the disease. This is a phenomenally high rate of incidence. The gene that causes it is dominant, which means that even if only one parent has the gene, the chances are that half the litter will not only inherit the gene but will have the disease. You can see how such a condition can become so prevalent so quickly.

For some time now there has been a scheme in place to try to screen for the condition. This consists of ultrasound scanning after ten months of age to look for the cysts and is roughly 98-per-cent accurate. There is also now a DNA test offered by the Animal Health Trust. This is fantastic news, as there are few diseases that could be so easy to get rid of. But is the screening compulsory in order to register a litter of Persians? No.

According to the CFA, there is no requirement to have any screening done for any genetic health disorders when registering cats or kittens. However, you'll be pleased to know that the section regarding genetic screening is very concerned with kittens showing coat colours or lengths that would normally not be accepted in the breed!

The GCCF is pleased to tell breeders that 'The GCCF says Health Comes First.' (Interestingly this is the *last* heading out of twelve in their list of important information for breeders). With respect to health testing for inherited disease it says:

'The GCCF is pleased that the increasing availability of genetic tests for hereditary diseases makes it possible for breeders to eliminate such diseases from their breeding lines. Where tests are available, the GCCF encourages the incorporation of their use into the registration policies for affected breeds.'

We will return to this shortly.

The fact is that the disease is also creeping into breeds that have Persian influence such as the Birman and Birmilla, and studies suggest that there is already a 14-per-cent incidence of the disease in the latter. It is very likely to have come from the Persian lines because the incidence in mixed-breed cats, that is, moggies is thought to be around 0.5 per cent.

A colleague of mine was talking to a Persian breeder about the disease and she was obviously concerned. He mentioned to her that screening was available and she was very keen to get it started and have her breeding cats scanned. However, once she realised that she could potentially lose 50 per cent of her available breeders she changed her mind and decided not to have the test done. This is not an uncommon scenario, no matter what the incidence of disease. Too often the look of the animal and its chance to do well at shows, and thus command good rates as a stud or for offspring, overrides the health of the animal. I've seen it many times and I believe it is wrong. Perhaps the GCCF would be wise to do more than *encourage* breeders to use available health tests and actually *make them compulsory.*

These disease rates raise the valid question of even further reducing the gene pool by excluding affected cats from breeding and that is a real concern where Persians and PKD are concerned. In order to get rid of the disease you would have to exclude half the cats and may well end up with other disease problems because of even narrower breeding. I don't know what the answer is but it seems to me that if a particular breed has such a level of potentially fatal, inherited disease we should consider whether to continue the breed. Most breeders are horrified at the idea of outbreeding. Outbreeding or outcrossing, is as it sounds, the opposite of inbreeding. Wikipedia defines it as: 'the practice of introducing unrelated genetic material into a breeding line. It increases genetic diversity, thus reducing the probability of diseases or other undesirable traits occurring due to genetic abnormalities.' In effect it would mean letting another breed be introduced to a number of matings to try to dilute the genetic material of the breed and reduce the frequency of inherited disease. Breeders do not like the idea because it is seen as 'soiling' the purity of their blood lines. However, we are at a point where it may end up being the only option because the pool is fast turning into stagnant sludge and some fresh, running water is desperately needed.

Another concern in our cats is heart disease. This is something we mentioned previously with regard to several dog breeds such as the Cavalier King Charles spaniel. Heart disease is also inheritable in cats. It is usually different to the type commonly seen in the dog. Affected cats tend to get very thickened heart walls. This, over time, has the effect of reducing how much blood can actually fit in the heart chambers. The walls also lose their elasticity and do not pump well. Eventually this can lead to death, although, as with the kidney disease, we do have excellent drugs now that can alleviate the symptoms. Unfortunately for some cats these drugs never get a chance because they may die before they show any signs of disease. The disease is usually seen in middle-aged to older cats but can occur as young as one year of age. I have already told you about the British shorthair breeder I knew who was devastated to find one of her young cats dead at the age of three from heart disease. Fortunately she was sensible enough to do something about it. This 'hypertrophic cardiomyopathy', or HCM, is listed as common in eight breeds by Gough and Thomas.

The disease can be shown up by ultrasound scanning but as yet the full nature of the inheritance is unknown. As a rule, it is wise to have breeding cats tested and not breed from those affected, but you will get some apparently normal cats that produce young with the disease so it may 'skip' generations. More work is being done to get to the bottom of it.

Cats can also suffer from hip dysplasia and luxating patellae, just as we saw in many dog breeds. Affected breeds include the Maine Coon, Persian and the Devon Rex.

Here are some other brief examples of inherited disease in cat breeds:

1. *Neuropathies*, or nerve disorders, in the Norwegian forest cat
2. *Alopecia*, or hair loss, in Birman, Burmese, Devon Rex and Siamese
3. *Myopathy*, or muscle weakness and collapse, in the Devon Rex, (these cats can also find it difficult to eat and swallow food.)
4. *Asthma* in Siamese cats
5. *Amyloidosis*, a potentially fatal disease in Abyssinians and Siamese.

There are also eye diseases causing blindness, immune diseases, endocrine diseases and various allergies that have all been shown to be inherited. Again, there is too much to go into in the remit of this book.

Suffice to say that, as cat breeds continue to be 'refined' by breeders after continual change and breed 'enhancement', these diseases will continue and become more common and new ones will be discovered.

PART FIVE

HOW DOES THE DREAM END?

The European Convention for the Protection of Pet Animals

This is a piece of legislation that has been knocking around since 1987 and to date eighteen countries have signed and ratified it. The convention looks at many aspects of pet animals but Article 5 concerns breeding. When you look at what the convention proposes you will see why what I say is true but you will also see why so many breeders in this country do not want us to sign it. Article 5 states that 'Any person who selects a pet animal for breeding shall be responsible for having regard to the anatomical, physiological and behavioural characteristics which are likely to put at risk the health and welfare of either the offspring or the female parent.'

Later, in 1995, a more detailed resolution on breeding was passed. Although this has no binding legal force, it basically recommends that cat and dog breed associations revise their breed standards to get rid of breed-related disorders and 'extreme characteristics detrimental to the health and welfare of the animals'. This resolution states (I rest my case) that the signatories are 'Convinced that these problems are related for a large part to the way breeding standards are formulated and interpreted'. It was also agreed that, 'If these measures are not sufficient, to consider the possibility of prohibiting the breeding and for phasing out the exhibition and the selling of certain types or breeds when characteristics of these animals correspond to harmful defects such as those presented in the Appendix.'

This is quite wordy but is the part that has caused most concern among the breeders of some dogs and cats with extreme characteristics. It effectively says that if you can't reform a breed standard sufficiently to make it healthy then that breed of dog or cat should effectively disappear. This could mean the end of the bulldog, chow, Persians, bassets, pugs, Shar Peis and so on. Now understandably people do not want this to happen and some changes are already underway.

169

The Kennel Club has tried hard to make the government see that they can control the problem and that we don't need to sign the convention. They have already reworded some of the breed standards to imply less exaggerated features. However, how long that will take to filter into the actual animals being bred remains to be seen. Moreover, to my mind, the proposed changes are very slight so will probably have little impact on the breeds' health.

What I find very disappointing is the total lack of participation from the UK. Veterinary representatives from Belgium, Denmark, Finland, Germany, Portugal, Sweden and Switzerland all participated and agreed the resolution. Even vets from countries not party to the Convention participated as observers (Italy, The Netherlands, Czech Republic, France, Hungary and the USA). The UK had no involvement at all. Many organisations were involved with the Convention in the role of expert observers, such as the Federation of Veterinarians of Europe, the International Cynologic Federation, the World Cat Federation, the International Feline Federation and the Governing Council of the Cat Fancy, among others. Maybe not quite so surprising is the fact that it did not include *any* of the kennel clubs of European countries.

Eighteen European countries have signed and ratified the Convention: Austria, Belgium, Bulgaria, Cyprus, Czech Republic, Denmark, Finland, France, Germany, Greece, Lithuania, Luxembourg, Norway, Portugal, Romania, Sweden, Switzerland and Turkey. Of these countries, eight signed and ratified the Convention with 'reservations', exempting them from certain articles, but *none of them* exempted themselves from Article 5 on breeding. A further two countries (Italy and The Netherlands) signed the Convention in 1987 but have not subsequently ratified it and Azerbaijan signed the Convention in 2003 but has not ratified it. The UK is not a signatory.

The breed characteristics that the Resolution considers so harmful that they need to be changed are:

- Extremes of size (large or small)
- Extreme shortness of skull and nose
- Extremes of back length compared to leg length
- Bowed or abnormally positioned legs
- Abnormally deep-set or protruding eyes
- Excessively long ears

- Skin folds
- Other extreme physical abnormalities such as hairless animals.

The Appendix to the Resolution provides very good evidence that these problems are a very real cause for concern worldwide as well as in the UK. I think it is worth reproducing them in full so you can see the major concerns:

The Parties strongly encourage cat and dog breeding associations to revise their breeding policies in the light of Article 5 of the Convention taking account in particular of the following guidelines:

Guidelines for the revision of breeding policies:
- set maximum and minimum values for height or weight of very large or small dogs, respectively, to avoid skeleton and joint disorders (e.g. dysplasia of hip joints or elbows, fractures, luxation of elbow or patella, persistent fontanella) and collapse of trachea;
- set maximum values for the proportion between length and height of short-legged dogs (e.g. Basset Hound, Dachshund) to avoid disorders of the vertebral column;
- set limits to the shortness of skull, especially nose, so that breathing difficulties and blockage of lachrymal ducts are avoided, as well as disposition to birth difficulties (e.g. Persian cats, especially the 'extreme type', Bulldogs, Japan Chin, King Charles Spaniel, Pug, Pekin Palacedog);
- prevent the occurrence of:
  - a persistent fontanella (e.g. Chihuahua) to avoid brain damages;
  - abnormal positions of legs (e.g. very steep line of hind legs in Chow Chow, Norwegian Buhund, Swedish Lapphund, Finnish Spitz; bowed legs in Basset Hound, Pekin Palacedog, Shi Tzu) to avoid difficulties in movement and joint degeneration;
  - abnormal positions of teeth (e.g. brachygnathia in Boxers, Bulldogs, Persian Cats) to avoid difficulties in feeding and caring for the newborn;
  - abnormal size and form of eyes or eyelids (e.g. ectropion: Basset Hound, Bloodhound, St Bernard; small deep lying

171

eyes with disposition to entropion: Airedale Terrier, Australian Terrier, Bedlington Terrier, Bullterrier, Bloodhound, Chow Chow, English Toy Terrier, Jagdterrier, Newfoundland, Shar Pei; large, protruding eyes: Boston Terrier, Cavalier King Charles Spaniel, Dandie Dinmont Terrier, Brussels Griffon, Japan Chin, King Charles Spaniel, Pug, Pekin Palacedog, Shi Tzu, Tibet Terrier) to avoid irritation, inflammation and degeneration as well as prolapse of eyes;
- very long ears (e.g. English Cocker Spaniel, Basset Hound, Bloodhound) to avoid disposition to injuries;
- markedly folded skin (e.g. Basset Hound, Bulldog, Bloodhound, Pug, Pekin Palacedog, Shar Pei) to avoid eczemas and in the case of furrows around the eyes irritation and inflammation of eyes;

- avoid or, if it is not possible to eliminate severe defects, discontinued breeding of:

  - animals carrying semi-lethal factors (e.g. Entlebucher Cattledog);
  - animals carrying recessive defect-genes (e.g. homozygotic Scottish Fold Cat: short legs, vertebral column and tail defects)
  - hairless dogs and cats (lack of protection against sun and chill, disposition to significant reduction of number of teeth, semi-lethal factor)
  - Manx-cat (movement disorder, disposition to vertebral column defects, difficulties in elimination of urine and faeces, semi-lethal factor)
  - cats carrying 'dominant white' (significant disposition to deafness);
  - dogs carrying 'Merle factor' (significant disposition to deafness and eye disorders, e.g.: Blue Merle Collie, Merle Sheltie, Merle Corgie, Merle Bobtail, Tigerdogge, Tigerteckel).

Note
The breeds mentioned in brackets are only examples in which these problems may occur.

Well, there you have it. Should the UK sign it? Of course we should. We shouldn't have any question in our minds as to whether we should sign it. We are effectively saying that we don't think it important to improve animal welfare or to stop breeding animals that experience ill health or actually suffer because of their breed standard. Where is it that the breed standard is most important? In the show ring.

So it is to the world of Crufts and other such circuses that we will now turn our attention.

There's No Business Like Show Business

How have we come to this point? How have we ended up in a situation where it is acceptable to design dogs and cats? I think it is even more apparent how far we've gone if you imagine doing it to another finely tuned species – the horse. Imagine if someone suddenly said that horses would look much better if they had extremely short legs for their size. Or that we should try to reduce the length of the head to create a 'heavily wrinkled' look. We would all find this totally unacceptable because it would effectively stop the animals from being able to perform as we expect them to.

When looked at it in this way I hope you can see why I feel the way I do. It has to stop. I'm not saying that we can't have breeds. I'm not saying that all pedigree breeds should be outlawed. I just want the extremes to be reversed. I do believe that some breeds can never be healthy and should be banned in their *current* form.

I want dogs and cats to be as healthy as they can be. I can't believe we have arrived at a point where the way a dog looks has become more important to us than its welfare. I'd like to tell you something someone once said to me. I can't say who because I can't prove it and I don't want to get sued, but suffice to say three other people witnessed it and I hope you will trust me enough to take my word for it. This person is someone very heavily involved with breeding and showing at quite a high level. We were having a fairly heated debate about pedigree health problems and he said to me that breeders' main concerns were type, temperament and health. Now when he said this I was a little shocked but thought he must have just presented them in no particular order. Just to be sure I asked him to clearly reiterate the point that those were the concerns *in that order*. He repeated again yes, health was number three, not only after temperament but looks. I said that I

174

thought it was appalling that anyone would care more about the way their animal looks than about its health and he simply changed the subject. If he's right then I'm on a hiding to nothing. I just hope that my suspicions that the majority of you *don't* feel that way are true.

I have terminally bored my family and friends with this subject and that is why I have written this book. I have become obsessed. Every time I see a breed of dog or cat I can't help going through a mental list in my head of what it is likely to be suffering from or what might cause its untimely death. I know there are many, many examples of all these dogs that have been lucky enough never to have any problems but I am telling you facts here. I have seen all of these problems countless times. I know there are many vets and many dog lovers who feel the same as I do. If pedigree dogs and cats didn't exist half the vets in this country would be out of a job. The fact is that the pedigree industry is enormous in this country and, indeed, throughout the world. At the centre of the industry is the showing world and this is something we need to carefully consider. Here I am not talking about fun shows in the local park or charity dos where someone gets a prize for having a waggy tail or for looking like their owner. I'm not talking about shows that demonstrate the incredible working abilities of our dogs. I'm talking about big, commercial, elitist, pedigree shows.

I have always felt uncomfortable about the reasons behind showing our dogs and cats. On the main page of the GCCF website there is a photograph of a beautiful cat. The title of the photograph says 'The Supreme Exhibit at the 2005 GCCF Supreme Show'. It sounds like an inanimate object, not someone's beloved pet, and this attitude is just one that I find unsettling about showing. I don't understand the psychology of it but I believe there is virtually no benefit for the animals involved. I know that many of you will say that your dog loves it and always wags his tail when he's finished in the ring. Of course he does, he's just had loads of praise. Any dog would wag his tail when he's called a good boy. I know many people say that shows are an excellent way to get your dog socialised and I'm sure this may be true in some cases. However, there are better ways to socialise your dog than a crowded, odd environment where none of the dogs are actually allowed off the lead or to play normally.

It is just so unnatural. Dogs should be out running about, getting muddy, playing and interacting. Cats should be climbing trees and watching the birds on the patio. Again, we are so used to seeing these shows and it is so traditional that we don't even stop to consider whether it is right or not. How long are we going to continue to use our pets as circus animals?

I suppose I've always subconsciously felt like this but it wasn't until I went to Crufts that I became so appalled. I was asked to go to Crufts a few years ago because we were on the television. Joe and I were asked to go and sign autographs on one of the stands. I felt quite uneasy about it and said I would go if I was in no way asked to endorse the show or pedigree breeding. I sold out basically; I put my ethics to one side because I needed the money. I'm glad in hindsight I did because I *can* now speak about it from personal experience and all the people who hate me for this cannot say I don't know what I'm talking about because I haven't been. In fact, I have been several times since to promote rescue dogs and various charities. I understand that Crufts is a very popular event for thousands of the public that are interested in dogs. It also has a role to play in education about dogs and a large number of charities do very well from a presence there. It is also a very good exhibition and commercial event for shops and bars, and fundamentally I believe a lot of people go there to mix with dog lovers. We are a nation of dog lovers, right? I understand all this but I do not believe it is a place to parade a beloved pet for hours on end in the hope of a rosette that the animal will have absolutely no comprehension of.

Crufts is one of the most enormous events I have ever seen. I remember thinking at the time, 'This is never going to stop. I will never be able to make a dent in this; it's just way too big.' I wandered round the place and became increasingly upset. The dogs that are there are kept in crates for the most of the day. I discovered that the ones that don't make the grade are not even allowed to go home early. They have to stay there. The reason for this, I discovered, is that the public must have their money's worth. They have paid to see all the dogs and see them they must, no matter what this means for the animals. In fairness a lot of the people that go probably don't know this. Next time you go just take a harder look at what's going on.

While I was there I heard the same announcement over and over again: would the owner of dog number whatever, please return to

176

your bay as your dog is in distress. This is supposed to be a place filled with animal lovers. How could there possibly be so many people that had allowed their dogs to become distressed? Perhaps it's because the whole place is daunting and distressing to many of the dogs there and when the one person they have a connection with wanders off to the bar for a natter and a pint the fear becomes a bit too much. Several people I've spoken to about this all agree. I'm not making this up.

The judging is tedious and relentless. The animals are examined time and again. I sit and watch it on the telly now and wonder why one of the dog's doesn't just turn savage in protest at someone grabbing its balls and looking at its teeth and trying to decide whether it is deformed and miserable enough to win a rosette. Cat showing is worse in a way. Many cats are not used to travelling and find physical restraint and handling extremely stressful. They are often not sociable animals by nature, so why on earth would we expect them to be 'happy' in a room full of hundreds of unfamiliar feline threats?

In my first job I had a client who bred standard poodles. He seemed very nice the first time I met him for a first vaccination for his eight-week-old puppy but during the whole time he was in the room he was constantly fiddling with the puppy, adjusting its feet and holding its head in a show position. I wanted to give him a clip round the ear and confiscate the dog. Puppies shouldn't be denied their puppyhood! Let him play and gambol as nature intended. It's akin to baby beauty pageants.

Do people actually think that their dog gives two hoots whether it is a good example of its breed or that it has any comprehension of what it means if it wins? Does it feel proud or is it just happy because its owner suddenly seems to be happy? Why must they be held with those tiny, thin leads wedged under their jaws and hauled round to keep their head held high? Why are their legs constantly adjusted to make them stand in the 'right' position? Why are they shampooed and groomed excessively so that all the natural oils are stripped out of their coats? Why do they have their hair tied back to keep it clean until show time? Why are small dogs put in cages to get from the car park to the hall in case they get dirty on the way, and why on earth are the animals not allowed to be neutered unless it is medically necessary?

I know the answer to this last question and it is the absolute crux of everything we have discussed. Top show winners 'should' be bred from because they are apparently the 'best' example of their breed. *But* this is based purely and totally on the way the animal looks and has *nothing* to do with its health. I sincerely doubt any vet would award best dog in the world to a Pekinese that appears to be in respiratory distress when asked to perform some light exercise. The top show winners may be morphologically pleasing and close to the breed standard, but it is *absolutely* no guarantee of good health or good health in the offspring. These champions then go on to sire multitudes of dogs and cats and so the inbreeding continues and any defective conformation or genetic makeup gaily gets passed along to their unfortunate young – all in the name of the breed standard.

I understand that lots of shows are very small-scale and fun. I also understand pride. I am incredibly proud of my dogs and I love it whenever anyone compliments me on how beautiful they are or how well behaved they are. I am happy to bathe in their reflected glory. I don't need a rosette to tell me how wonderful they are; every second I'm with them does that.

I know loads of you don't take it too seriously and I know it's a nice day out and you're not that bothered if you don't win anything, but just take a minute to stop and consider what your dog or cat would prefer. Why not take it for an extra long walk or five more minutes play with a catnip toy instead – something that you can both enjoy.

From Small Beginnings...

These animals are our companions. They love us unconditionally and they have a right to be respected by us. They have a right to expect us to love them unconditionally too, whether they are a good example of a breed or 'just' a mutt. How can we possibly say that any dog is better than another? They are all just dogs, aren't they?

As the years have gone by I have come to realise that I am not the only one that feels like this and I am in a position to make some people listen. If I don't make the most of the fact that I am slightly well known to the animal-lovers of this country, then I have wasted every minute that I have devoted to achieving my goal. I am in a position to help thousands more animals than I could by just being a general practitioner, and no matter how small a difference that turns out to be it will be worth it. From small beginnings come great things. Isn't that what they say? The truth is that I will never be happy in my work if I keep this to myself and nothing would ever change if everyone thought, 'I can't make a difference so there's no point trying.'

What should we do now? I hope that by now you are at least a little indignant about what is going on, if not outraged. So what are we going to do? If we carry on breeding as we are at the moment, then these animals could become completely non-viable. As I mentioned before, without intervention these breeds would die out, but if we continue they will literally be bred to extinction. Mother Nature has been helping things survive for millennia and we have completely gone against everything she would do. I have some ideas and, if we stick together, maybe, just maybe, things might get a little better. Here they are:

1. If you want a pet, look into it before you buy it. Find out as much information as you can. Go to your vet and try

179

to get a clear idea of what to look for, how much to pay and what to expect. Whatever animal, no matter how big or small, consider whether you can look after it properly.

2. If you're thinking of having the odd litter from your dog or cat, or if you are the most serious and dedicated breeder known to man, then do the same – look into *all* the potential diseases and health schemes that are available. It is no longer acceptable to have a blasé attitude about this and think, 'Oh well, we'll just risk it, it'll probably be all right.' These diseases will never stop until we start acting responsibly. I don't care if your cat is Danny-Champion-of-the-bloody-World; if he carries PKD don't breed from him!

3. Write to the Kennel Club, the Governing Council of the Cat Fancy and the Cat Fanciers' Association and demand to know why health tests that have been proven to reduce inherited disease are not compulsory and why they feel the need to keep making the conformation of breeds more and more exaggerated. At the very least we should expect show champions to have to undergo rigorous health tests and screens *and pass them* before they are allowed to be bred from.

4. Good, responsible breeders and vets should work together. Let's have a BVA/BSAVA recommended breeders list. This would include not only breeders whose dogs have had and passed all health tests but would also ensure correct advice on topics such as vaccination, worming and diet. Many vets still see numerous owners who have been given spurious advice regarding all these issues.

5. When you buy a pedigree animal the fact that it comes from a line of show winners based on body shape does not necessarily mean you will be buying a healthy animal. Ask the breeder about health tests and ask to see the results. Go armed with the facts and don't be afraid to question before you buy. And remember, just because a breed may not have been mentioned in this book, does not mean it is free from disease. This book is not exhaustive.

6. We should follow the lead that Australia has shown. Their Listing of Inherited Disorders in Animals (LIDA, http://www.vetsci.usyd.edu.au/lida/) database lets people search animal breeds to see the diseases they can experience and has easy-to-understand descriptions of these problems. They also have many vets on board to continue the monitoring of these conditions and keep an audit on-going.

7. I'd like to see the governing bodies of pedigree cats and dogs do more to ensure positive identification of animals to prevent fraud. All pedigrees should be permanently identified by means such as microchipping. This would help stop animals being sold, presumed to be from one particular sire or dam, only to find out later that is not the case. This would also make it easier to track disease prevalence in certain lines and highlight where outbreeding should be considered most urgently.

8. If you want a breed of dog that has always been traditionally docked, don't accept one. While we wait for the new legislation to come into force you might struggle to find one undocked. Be demanding and persevere. The sooner we get used to seeing these animals in all their glory the better. When breeders realise they *can* sell dogs with tails things will begin to change.

9. I'd like advertisers to be responsible too. I'd like to see a Dulux Old English sheepdog with an undocked tail and I'd like to see cosmetic companies stop using things like Shar-Pei puppies to advertise anti-wrinkle creams. I'd like dog magazines that profile breeds to stop showing photographs of docked dogs completely. We have to stop viewing docked dogs as the norm.

10. If you think your dog or cat is beautiful then delight in looking at it, invite your friends over to look at it if you like. Why haul it all over the country and the world to show it to other people in a completely unnatural environment? If you want a doll, buy one. If you want

to exhibit, buy an antique car to polish; if you like backcombing and using hairspray, train to be a hairdresser!

11. I'd like the BBC to stop glamorising the suffering every year with their fluffy portrayal of Crufts, or at least let's see some good documentaries about the problems these animals have to balance the coverage.

12. Perhaps most importantly, if you would like a pet please consider an abandoned one. There are thousands of beautiful cats and dogs waiting for deserving homes in rescue centres all over the country. There are plenty of breed rescues as well if you would like a certain breed. Even if you're pretty sure you don't want a mutt or a moggie, go and have a look anyway, you might be surprised how quickly they steal your heart.

So there it is, the bare bones of it. I have done my part but now it is up to all of you to take up the baton. I hope I have made you chuckle; maybe some of you have cried with me. But more than anything I hope a lot of you are angry enough to do something about it. Thanks for taking the time to listen and here's hoping the dream has a happy ending.

Me and the boys.
© Nikki English

References

Peter Bedford, 'Ocular disease in the cat', *In Practice*, March 1983, vol. 5, pp. 64–70.

Peter Bedford, 'Ophthalmic surgery in the dog and cat', *In Practice*, July 1980, vol. 2, pp. 5–14.

D.C. Blood and V.P. Studdert, *'Bailliere's Comprehensive Veterinary Dictionary'*, Bailliere and Tindall 1990.

British Veterinary Association/Kennel Club Hip Dysplasia Scheme – Breed Mean Scores at 01/01/06 (London, BVA Publications, 2006).

Carolyn Burton, 'Surgical diseases of the trachea in the dog and cat', *In Practice*, Oct 2003, vol. 25, pp. 514–27.

M.J. Cannon et al, 'Prevalence of polycystic kidney disease in Persian cats in the United Kingdom', *Veterinary Record*, Oct 2001, vol. 149, pp. 409–11.

Dr Sheila Crispin et al, 'Hereditary Eye Disease and the BVA/KC/ISDS Eye Scheme', *In Practice*, June 1995, vol. 17, pp. 254–64.

Jean Dodds, 'Inherited coagulation disorders in the dog', *In Practice*, March 1983, vol. 5, pp. 54–8.

Joanna Dukes McEwan 'Canine dilated cardiomyopathy 1. Breed manifestations and diagnosis', *In Practice*, 2000, vol. 22, pp. 520–30.

Darren Foster, 'Diagnosis and management of chronic coughing in cats', *In Practice*, May 1998, vol. 20, pp. 261–7.

G. Gandini et al, 'Cerebellar cortical degeneration in three English bulldogs: clinical and neuropathological findings', *Journal of Small Animal Practice*, vol. 2005, 46, pp. 291–4.

Alex Gough and Alison Thomas, 'Breed Predispositions to Disease in Dogs and Cats' (Oxford, Blackwell Science, 2004).

The Kennel Club, *Illustrated Breed Standards* (London, Ebury Press, 2003).

Amy MacKay, 'Practical approach to the dyspnoeic cat', *In Practice*, April 2001, vol. 23, pp. 198–207.

P.D. McGreevy and F.W. Nicholas, 'Some Practical Solutions to Welfare Problems in Dog Breeding', *Animal Welfare* 1999.

Malcolm McKee, 'Intervertebral disc disease in the dog 1. Pathophysiology and diagnosis', *In Practice*, July 2000, vol. 22, pp. 355–69.

A.R. Michell, 'Longevity of British breeds of dog and its relationships with sex, size, cardiovascular variables and disease', *Veterinary Record*, Nov 1999, vol. 145, pp. 625–9.

Simon Platt and Natasha Olby, '*BSAVA Manual of Canine and Feline Neurology*', 2004.

C.M. Poncet et al, 'Prevalence of Gastrointestinal Tract Lesions in 73 Brachycephalic Dogs with Upper Airway Syndrome', *Journal of Small Animal Practice*, 2005, 46, pp. 273–9.

Clare Rusbridge, 'Neurological Diseases of the Cavalier King Charles Spaniel', *Journal of Small Animal Practice*, 2005, vol. 46, pp. 265–72.

Clare Rusbridge as quoted by Jayne Newton 'Breeders' bid to eliminate SM draws mixed reaction', *Vet Times*, 2006, vol. 36, no. 26, page 2.

Dr Jeff Sampson, 'The Geneticist's View on Dog Breeding; How Can Improved Health be Achieved?', *The European Journal of Companion Animal Practice*, April 2005, vol. 15.

Michael Schaer, *Clinical Medicine of the Dog and Cat* (London, Manson Publishing, 2003).

Paul Smith, 'Management of chronic degenerative mitral valve disease in dogs', *In Practice,* July 2006, vol. 28, pp. 376–83.

Mike Stockman, 'Inheritable defects in dogs:1', *In Practice*, Nov 1982, vol. 4, pp. 170–75.

Keith Thoday, 'Skin diseases of the cat', *In Practice*, Nov 1981, vol. 3, pp. 22–35.

Jacky Turner (on behalf of Advocates for Animals), *The Price of a Pedigree* (Advocates for Animals, 2006).

K. Vermeersch et al, 'Sensory Neuropathy in Two Border Collie Puppies', *Journal of Small Animal Practice*, 2005, vol. 46, pp. 295–9.

Dr Malcolm B. Willis BSc PhD as quoted on www.gsdleague.co.uk/hd.htm 2000

Kim Willoughby, 'Differential diagnosis of nasal disease in cats', *In Practice*, April 1995, vol. 17, pp. 154–61.

Web sources

Report of the meeting of the Multilateral Consultation on the European Convention for the Protection of Pet Animals (ETS 125), 1995 Available at http://www.dspace.dial.pipex.com/town/plaza/jb60/felinewelfare/coemcp.htm

Information on original Twisty Kats found at www.karmafarms.com/twisty.htm

Quotes from CFA found at www.cfainc.org

Definition of outcrossing found at http://en.wikipedia.org/wiki/Outcrossing

Useful Website Addresses

Information on health schemes and breed disease

Animal Health Trust:
    www.aht.org.uk/sci_diag_genetics_dna.html
British Veterinary Association:
    www.bva.co.uk/public/chs/eye_scheme.asp
    www.bva.co.uk/public/chs/elbow_scheme.asp
    www.bva.co.uk/public/chs/hip_scheme.asp
German shepherd dog league:
    www.gsdleague.co.uk/hd.htm
Kennel Club:
    www.thekennelclub.org.uk/item/308
    www.thekennelclub.org.uk/item/314
University of Sydney:
    www.vetsci.usyd.edu.au/lida/
The Cavalier King Charles spaniel club:
    www.thecavalierclub.co.uk/health/hearts/proposal06.html

Major Animal Rescue and Rehoming Charities

Dogs Trust:
    www.dogstrust.org.uk/
The Blue Cross:
    www.bluecross.org.uk
Battersea Dogs and Cats Home:
    www.dogshome.org

Royal Society for the Prevention of Cruelty to Animals:
www.rspca.org.uk
Wood Green Animal Shelters:
www.woodgreen.org.uk
Cats Protection:
www.cats.org.uk
National Animal Welfare Trust:
www.nawt.org.uk

Information for prospective vet students

UCAS:
www.ucas.com
Bristol University:
www.vetschool.bris.ac.uk/
Glasgow University:
www.gla.ac.uk/faculties/vet/
Edinburgh University:
www.vet.ed.ac.uk/
Royal Veterinary College London:
www.rvc.ac.uk/
Liverpool University:
www.liv.ac.uk/vets/
Cambridge University:
www.vet.cam.ac.uk/
University College Dublin:
www.ucd.ie/agfoodvet/index.html
Nottingham University:
www.nottingham.ac.uk/vet/

Information on the European Convention for the Protection of Pet Animals

http://conventions.coe.int/Treaty/en/Treaties/Html/125.htm
http://en.wikipedia.org/wiki/European_Convention_for_the_Protection_of_Pet_Animals
http://www.dspace.dial.pipex.com/town/plaza/jb60/felinewelfare/coe
mcp.htm

Miscellaneous

Contact Emma Milne:
    www.emmathevet.co.uk
Vets Against Docking:
    www.vetsagainstdocking.co.uk
The Royal College of Veterinary Surgeons:
    www.rcvs.org.uk/
British Small Animal Veterinary Association:
    www.bsava.com/
British Veterinary Association:
    www.bva.co.uk/
Governing Council of the Cat Fancy:
    www.gccfcats.org/
The Kennel Club:
    www.thekennelclub.org.uk
Cat bed/carrier mentioned in cat section: www.petzaporter.com

Acknowledgements

Thanks to the following for their valuable contributions to this book:

Dr David Gould BSc(Hons) BVM&S PhD MRCVS DVOphthal DipECVO for the use of photographs.

Andrew Moores BVSc DSAS(Orth) DipECVS MRCVS for the use of photographs

Mr and Mrs Carmichael for use of the photographs of Caffreys, the beautiful, undocked boxer who I know is dearly missed.

Jacky Turner and Advocates for Animals for the research into the European Convention for the Protection of Pet Animals

RSPCA for use of photographs

Dr Paul McGreevy BVSc PhD MRCVS MACVS Cert CABC Grad Cert Higher Ed for general advice and for highlighting LIDA as a source of information

Mark Goodman BVM&S MRCVS for anecdotal evidence and use of photographs

Tanya Banks for use of photographs of Buster

Julian and Melissa Bainbridge for use of photographs of Jim

Mrs Randall for use of photographs of Sophie

Mrs Reed for use of photographs of Wat Tyler

Alison Jones BVetMed MRCVS for use of photograph of Portia

Book Guild Publishing for 'taking a punt'.